7 80 mc

D0845824

THOMAS
TRAHERNE

Mystical Symbolism

in the poetry

of

THOMAS TRAHERNE

by

Alison J. Sherrington

UNIVERSITY
OF
QUEENSLAND PRESS

© University of Queensland Press, St. Lucia, Queensland, 1970
Registered in Australia for transmission by post as a book
Text set in Monotype Garamond 11/11 and printed on Burnie Feather-
weight Book 70/g.s.m. by The Wilke Group Pty. Ltd., Zillmere, Brisbane
Bound by Stanley Owen and Sons Pty. Ltd., Alexandria, New South Wales
National Library of Australia Registry Number Aus 68-3291
Distributed by International Scholarly Book Services, Inc. Great Britain-
Europe-North America
SBN 7022 0578 8
Designed by Cyrelle

PREFACE

WHAT FIRST IMPRESSES THE READER OF THOMAS TRAHERNE'S poems is the unity of vision which they express; they have a personal quality which is remarkably distinctive. As is inevitable in mystical writing, Traherne uses earthly symbols to represent heavenly things, but his symbolism seems unremarkable on the surface, and its sources are obviously conventional. Why, then, does his poetry seem so fresh, so original? One of the answers to this question must lie in the particular use which Traherne makes of conventional mystical symbolism. Although in most of the following pages my immediate concern is with symbolic meanings, my ultimate aim is to make a contribution towards the understanding of Traherne as an artist. Only when one is aware of the distinctions of meaning involved in a poet's use of symbols can one fully appreciate his poems as poems.

Mystical symbolism is an attempt to express, by means of analogy, experiences and ideas not directly expressible in words. Since most people have known flashes of rudimentary vision, an immense part of general literature is tinged with mystical feeling. Many poets who are not mystics have written poems which could be called mystical because of the use of symbols to suggest intimations of a consciousness wider and deeper than the normal. One would perhaps hesitate to call Shelley a mystic, yet I believe one would be justified in calling poems like *Hymn to Intellectual Beauty* mystical. The validity of a study of Traherne's mystical symbolism does not depend, therefore, on whether this seventeenth-century poet can properly be called a mystic.

Nevertheless, although some critics hesitate to attribute to Traherne actual mystical experience, I have used the term "mystic" in reference to him in this study, because the discovery in 1964 of the Osborn Manuscript containing Traherne's *Select Meditations* leaves no doubt in my mind that he was indeed a mystic. In one of these meditations (IV, 3), Traherne speaks openly of his personal experience:

This Endless Comprehension of my Immortal Soul when I first saw it, so wholy Ravished and Transported my spirit, that for a fortnight after I could scarsly Think or speak or write of any other Thing. But Like a man Doteing with Delight and Extasie, Talk of it Night and Day as if all the Joy of Heaven and Earth were Shut up in it. For in very Deed there I saw the Divine Image Relucent and Shining, There I saw the foundation of mans Excellency, and that which made Him a Son of God. Nor ever shall I be able to forget its Glory.[1]

Even though Traherne here describes the "Endless Comprehension" of his soul rather than of God, this experience must have resulted from intimacy with the Divine.

For several reasons I decided to approach the study of Traherne's symbolism through his poetry. Some of his prose works are still unobtainable or even unpublished, while all the poems known to be his are readily available. Nevertheless there is a greater need for a study of Traherne's poems than for a study of his obtainable prose passages, for the prose of *Centuries of Meditations* is acknowledged to be his greatest work, and he is consequently better known as a prose writer than as a poet. Indeed, those critics who deal with Traherne as an artist tend to dismiss his poetry lightly in order to concentrate their attention on the beauty of his prose style.[2]

Traherne's work entitled *A Serious and Pathetical Contemplation of the Mercies of God, in several most Devout and Sublime Thanksgivings for the Same*, presents a problem for the critic because of its originality of form. These *Thanksgivings* are little-known poems in a type of rhythmical prose which seems to me to be the writer's most natural and characteristic medium of expression. Although I agree with H. M. Margoliouth that they were "written by Traherne not as prose but as unconventional poetry",[3] I have excluded them from the material used for this study, apart from the three passages of rhymed poetry which they contain.

The poems from the Dobell Folio Manuscript, the *Poems of Felicity*, and the rhymed passages from the *Thanksgivings*, together

---

1. Quoted by Louis L. Martz in *The Paradise Within: Studies in Vaughan, Traherne, and Milton* (New Haven and London, 1964), p. 210.
2. Notable exceptions are Q. Iredale, Gladys I. Wade, K. W. Salter, Helen C. White, Robert Ellrodt, and A. L. Clements.
3. H. M. Margoliouth (ed.), *Thomas Traherne: Centuries, Poems, and Thanksgivings* (2 vols.; Oxford, 1958), I, ix–x.

with the few poems from the *Centuries* and *Christian Ethicks*, *An Hymne upon St Bartholomews Day* from the Church's Year Book, and the early verse from Philip Traherne's Notebook, must be considered. I have excluded from the material used for this work Traherne's three verse translations of Latin poems, and also the six poems from *Meditations on the Six Days of the Creation*. Traherne's authorship of the latter has not been proved conclusively,[4] and I am all the more cautious since five verse passages from Philip Traherne's Notebook which were attributed to Thomas Traherne and printed in Margoliouth's edition have recently been proved to be the work of other authors.[5] These five passages are *a Serious and a Curious night-Meditation*, and those beginning "What e're I have from God alone I have", "Oh how injurious is this wall of sin", "As fragrant Mirrhe within the bosom hid", and "To bee a Monarch is a glorious thing".

Some explanation is needed of the textual difficulties facing the student of Traherne's poetry. Twenty-two of the poems from Thomas Traherne's Dobell Folio Manuscript and the poem *On News* from the *Centuries* are also found in an altered and generally inferior form in the volume which his brother Philip prepared for the press with the title *Poems of Felicity*, and it is certain that the other thirty-eight poems in Philip's volume are not altogether as Thomas left them. Moreover, Philip made some changes in the Dobell Folio Manuscript itself. H. M. Margoliouth has restored Thomas's own text wherever possible, and it is his edition[6] which I have used for this study. When Philip's version of a poem is printed as well as Thomas's original, I have considered only the original version. Sometimes two versions by Thomas are available; for example, an earlier form of *The Approach* appears in the *Centuries* and a later and improved form in the Dobell Folio Manuscript. When an earlier and a later version, both unchanged by Philip, are printed, I have preferred the later version. Traherne's underlining is reproduced by italics, and I have also been careful to copy his spelling, capitalization, and punctuation accurately, even though his punctuation is sometimes illogical, as in these lines from the first stanza of *Eden*:

---

4. See Margoliouth, *op. cit.*, I, xvi–xvii.
5. See Anne Ridler (ed.), *Thomas Traherne: Poems, Centuries and Three Thanksgivings* (London, 1966), p. xv.
6. *Thomas Traherne: Centuries, Poems, and Thanksgivings* (2 vols.; Oxford, 1958).

A learned and a Happy Ignorance
Divided me,
From all the Vanitie,
From all the Sloth Care Pain and Sorrow that advance,
The madness and the Miserie
Of Men.

I should like to thank all those who have helped me with my work in any way. I am chiefly indebted to Professor K. G. Hamilton and to Dr. Beverley Sherry for their valuable suggestions, and to the staff of the Main Library of the University of Queensland for their courteous efficiency in procuring material for me.

A. J. S.
University of Queensland
1968

CONTENTS

INTRODUCTION

"THE AUTHOR
TO THE CRITICAL PERUSER"

POETRY REDEEMS FROM DECAY THE VISITATIONS OF THE DIVINITY IN MAN. (SHELLEY: *A Defence of Poetry*)

THIS WORK IS PRIMARILY A STUDY OF TRAHERNE'S USE OF symbols in his poetry, both the significance which he gives to traditional symbols and the aesthetic result of his symbolic vision. The relationships between symbols are explored to reveal the emotive and intellectual pattern creating that unity of personal vision which is so impressive in the work of this mystic and which is directly reflected in his literary style. The ideas in Traherne's introductory poem, *The Author to the Critical Peruser*, are used as a framework for most of this Introduction; the first seven chapters bear the names of his key symbols— Senses, Light, Water, Space, Child, King, Marriage—and each deals with an important group of symbols, showing the links connecting the symbols within the group, and the links connecting the group to other groups; the final chapter—Traherne, Symbolist and Poet—is concerned with artistic considerations associated with the poet's use of mystical symbolism; while the Conclusion, by showing the workings of Traherne's chief spiritual impulse, the passion for the infinite, in his most comprehensive poem, *My Spirit*, recapitulates and clarifies the main points which have been made in the previous sections.

The greatest difficulty encountered in the writing of this book was the necessity to include a large number of quotations from Traherne's poems, since quotations, if not handled very skilfully, might interrupt the flow of the thought and make the style disjointed. However, for two reasons there seemed no way of reducing their number. Firstly, a study of his symbolism demands illustration from the actual text of his poems, and they are so

1

little known that the reader might be greatly inconvenienced if he were constantly confronted with mere references to them. Secondly, as Traherne seldom constructs a whole poem or even a lengthy section of a poem around a particular symbol, it was often necessary to quote many short sections from different poems instead of one longer passage in order to present an adequate picture of all the facets of his use of one symbol.

Hitherto, most critics have confined themselves to a discussion of Traherne's philosophical and mystical ideas, virtually excluding specific consideration of him as a symbolist or as a poet. The occasional comments on the literary quality of his writing are generally limited to statements about the inferiority of his poetry to his prose, the simplicity of his style, and the technical deficiencies of his verse.[1] Some critics, in the course of a discussion of his philosophy, mention that the symbolic use of the sphere, the sun, the human eye, and the mirror is derived from Plato and Plotinus; but the only symbol whose meaning has been explored in any detail is the child, the most obvious of the symbols which are fundamental to Traherne's mysticism. There has as yet been no attempt to make a close study of the whole pattern of Traherne's mystical symbolism and thus to see deeply into the unity of spiritual impulse which, once discovered, illuminates even the most prosaic lines of verse and enriches the reader's literary appreciation of Traherne's writing. A convenient starting point for such a study is provided by *The Author to the Critical Peruser*, in which the poet states his aesthetic theory and justifies it by relating it to his philosophical and mystical ideas. Traherne tells his reader that his poems are written

> to th'end thy Soul might see
> With open Eys thy Great *Felicity*,
> Its Objects view, and trace the glorious Way
> Wherby thou may'st thy Highest Bliss enjoy.

There is thus no doubt that the didacticism of his poetry, like that of any serious seventeenth-century poetry, is considered a justification of its existence. But Traherne's aim is a very daring one, for the subject which he claims to teach is Felicity, and his one criticism of the education which he received at Oxford is that "There was never a Tutor that did professely Teach Felicity: tho

---

1. Except, notably, in the criticism by Q. Iredale, Gladys I. Wade, K. W. Salter, Helen C. White, Robert Ellrodt, and A. L. Clements.

that be the Mistress of all other Sciences".[2] Traherne believes that he has something new and important to say, something that will fill a major gap in human knowledge:

> But then, Where is? What is, Felicity?
> Here all Men are in doubt,
> And unresolv'd, they cannot speak,
> What 'tis.[3]

Even in his short direct statement of his didactic purpose,[4] Traherne's ecstatic enthusiasm for his subject is evident. Man's Felicity is "Great", he is capable of enjoying "Highest Bliss", and the way to it is "glorious". The tone of this introductory poem is that of the mystic and prophet who writes primarily because he must express his experiences and share them with others, not that of the pious clergyman writing merely because he feels it his duty to teach his flock. Traherne himself says that he wrote *Christian Ethicks* because he was "in danger of bursting" with the joy of his discoveries about life;[5] and he declares in the *Centuries* that "you never Enjoy the World aright, till you so lov the Beauty of Enjoying it, that you are Covetous and Earnest to Persuade others to Enjoy it" (I, 31). The missionary fervour of his writing is therefore of a peculiarly personal kind, a "bursting forth of a violent inner energy".[6]

In *The Author to the Critical Peruser*, Traherne states not only his didactic purpose but also his aesthetic ideal. As a teacher, his aim is to show the reader his Felicity; as a poet, his aim is to show the "naked Truth". This virtual identification of Felicity with Truth is a subtle introduction to the rich associations which the word "Felicity" has for the poet. The student of his writings gradually realizes that he uses it to cover a wide range of meanings associated with the idea of true blessedness, and that when charged with its full significance, as in the poem *Felicity*, it becomes synonymous with "God". However, the chief point which is made in the first verse-paragraph of his opening poem is that since "A Sight of Happiness is Happiness"[7] and the reader's enjoyment of "Highest Bliss" is dependent on his ability to see

---

2. *Centuries* III, 37.
3. *Dissatisfaction*, ll. 66-69.
4. *The Author to the Critical Peruser*, ll. 7-10.
5. Gladys I. Wade, *Thomas Traherne: A Critical Biography* (Princeton, 1944), p. 138.
6. *Ibid.*, p. 138.
7. *Centuries* III, 60.

"With open Eys" his "Great *Felicity*", clear vision of Truth is the supreme necessity of life, and plain expression of Truth the highest purpose of didactic art.

For Traherne, the true poet is one who sees Truth naked and presents it naked, though "in many faces shewn" (l. 1). He is one who leads his reader to find the One in the many, to share his vision of God immanent in all things and of all things thus united in God. Felicity is waiting to be seen and enjoyed by the viewing of its "Objects", and Traherne claims that since he is one of those "very few" who have "known" Truth's "inward Beauties", the "Excellence" of his verse is that it

> Brings down the highest Mysteries to sense
> And keeps them there.

These "highest Mysteries" are "Mountains" which must be made "plain" (l. 4) so that the reader might grasp them with his "sense".

In his introductory poem, Traherne takes great care to describe his poetic method. The plain expression of Truth demands the use of "transparent Words, a Strain / That lowly creeps"; true poetry is a simple, unpretentious reflection of the pure gold, the "real Crowns and Thrones and Diadems", of the poet's vision. He rejects the "Superficial Gems" of conventional poetical ornament—the "curling Metaphors that gild the Sence"[8] and the "*Zamzummim* words" that "will not make us wise". He thinks it best to omit references to strange oracles or religions, which, however interesting, would be unprofitable for his purpose; he also chooses to avoid imitation of the classics, "The Streams that flow from high *Parnassus* hill". Any artificiality or affectation would spoil his

> easy Stile drawn from a native vein,
> A clearer Stream than that which Poets feign,
> Whose bottom may, how deep so'ere, be seen.

Although Traherne's search for a plain style leads him to sweep aside many of the poetic conventions of his day, it is

---

8. This is a direct reference to l. 5 of Herbert's poem, *Jordan* II. It may be noted here that, in the seventeenth century, statements about the virtues of simplicity were very common, but it will become clear that Traherne's conscious search for simplicity is inspired by a different feeling from Herbert's fear of weaving himself into the sense (*Jordan* II, l. 14) or Marvell's awareness of the "wreaths of Fame and Interest" (*The Coronet*, l. 16).

evident even in this poem that he accepts the use of simple conventional symbols; for example, the naked expression of Truth is the "Simple Light" needed to guide the reader along "the glorious Way". Since mysticism consists in an experience which is in the most literal sense ineffable, the use of symbols is inevitable in mystical writing, and conventional ones would be those most clearly understood by the reader.

Traherne's passion for Felicity and his consequent desire for clear vision results not only in the use of a plain style of writing but also in the exaltation of man. Man must indeed be a glorious creature, since he is capable of seeing and thus possessing Felicity. Traherne's statement that in his poems the reader will find

> No florid Streams of Superficial Gems,
> But real Crowns and Thrones and Diadems!

introduces the idea of the happy man, the man with right values, as a spiritually wealthy king, and the poet makes a very bold claim for the didactic purpose of his verse when he declares:

> To make us Kings indeed! Not verbal Ones,
> But reall Kings, exalted unto Thrones;
> And more than Golden Thrones! 'Tis this I do,
> Letting Poëtick Strains and Shadows go.

This is one example of how Traherne's fresh insight into man's exalted position in the universe often leads him to use conventional symbols in an unexpected way. In mystical literature it is more usual to refer to God as a King, but here the king symbol is used of man instead.

The last three verse-paragraphs of *The Author to the Critical Peruser* are devoted to an analogy between the "idle Fancies, Toys, and Words" which most poets employ to "gild the Sence", often in an attempt to hide worthless thoughts ("Like gilded Scabbards hiding rusty Swords"), and the "rich Attire" which "vulgar Souls" admire instead of "God's diviner Works". It is significant that by this analogy the "inward Beauties" of "naked Truth" are compared with the "Beauty" of the naked body and mind (or soul) of man, and the "Superficial Gems" of "painted Eloquence" are compared with "His Rings, his precious Stones, his Gold and Plate" (l. 40) which are falsely valued above real gems such as his "useful Eys", "precious Hands", "polisht Flesh", and "saphire Veins" (ll. 46–49). But though man's body is "divine" (ll. 47, 64) and "Of glorious worth" (l. 54), his soul is the most precious gem of all, for in its

> concealed Face,
> Which comprehendeth all unbounded Space,
> GOD may be seen,

and it can "view *Eternity*" as well as Infinity ("all unbounded Space"), for these are really the same. Truth, Felicity, Bliss, Eternity, Infinity—all are different names for the one God Who may be seen and enjoyed by the man who has become a king by the spiritual possession of "real Crowns and Thrones and Diadems" such as his own body and soul.

Traherne's highest proof that man is made in the image of God is offered by his statement that man's soul "comprehendeth all unbounded Space". This, then, is man's greatest glory, his highest attainment of Felicity. As one studies the works of this poet, it becomes more and more evident that his passion for Felicity is in fact a passion for the infinite, the unbounded, in everything; and, as has already been shown, it is this spiritual impulse which is at the root of Traherne's desire for that clear vision by which the "Highest Bliss" might be enjoyed. One might sum up thus the two important consequences of such a desire for himself and for his reader: he deliberately chooses a naked style of writing which demands the use of simple mystical symbols drawn from conventional sources; he also presents a picture of man as an exalted creature capable of seeing and thus possessing the Infinite, and this necessitates a frequently original use of these conventional symbols.

The reader finds in Traherne's introductory poem a fore-shadowing of five groups of symbols which are important for an understanding of his poetry, and whose meanings are explored in the following chapters under the headings of Senses, Light, Water, Space, and King. The eyes of the soul, declares the mystic, need "A Simple Light", "A clearer Stream than that which Poets feign" (l. 18), to comprehend "all unbounded Space" and make man a king. The child and marriage symbols are not directly used here, but their very close relationship with all of Traherne's other groups of symbols will be demonstrated in this study. Thus *The Author to the Critical Peruser* provides the reader not only with a very valuable introduction to Traherne's basic assumptions about life and art, but also with a key to his whole pattern of symbols.

I

SENSES

IT IS HE THAT IS THE EYE OF MY MIND.
(HERMES TO TAT)

SOME OF THE MOST STRIKING STATEMENTS IN *The Author to the Critical Peruser* are those in which the faculty of sight is used as a symbol for a spiritual faculty. Traherne says that his poems are written

> to th'end thy Soul might see
> With open Eyes thy Great *Felicity*,

and that in this soul of man, which can "view *Eternity*" (l. 60), "GOD may be seen". It is clear even in his introductory poem that Traherne, like all other mystics, believes that there is a mystical analogy between the spiritual and the sensory realms, and that

> it is possible . . . to speak of inner experiences which some-how seem analogous to one or another of the five types of sensory experience, and yet which do not consist in the re-presentation of any sensory experience, whether in hallucination or in imagination.[1]

The study of the distinctions of meaning involved in Traherne's choice of a particular physical sense to symbolize the quality of a particular experience is an interesting one.

Mystics generally express their experiences in terms of sight, which has always been regarded as the highest and most "spiritual" of the physical senses because it "not only demands no contact with the thing seen, but asks not even that the object shall be a source of vibrations. It need only be a reflector of

---

1. Mary Anita Ewer, *A Survey of Mystical Symbolism* (London, 1933), p. 35.

7

them."[2] *The Vision* is one of those poems in which Traherne deals specifically with the importance of the exercise of spiritual sight in the attainment of Felicity.

The opening statement that "Flight is but the Preparative" links *The Vision* with the preceding poems in the Dobell Folio Manuscript. In *The Preparative* the poet states that since "Felicitie / Appears to none but them that purely see"[3] and false values corrupt the sight and fetter the mind (stanza 5), the recovery of pure vision and true freedom, the preparation for Felicity, demands a "Flight" from the tainted environment of the world of mankind: "My Soul retire, / Get free." The first lines of *The Instruction* show that this "Flight" involves an abjuration of the flesh:

> Spue out thy filth, thy flesh abjure;
> Let not Contingents thee defile.

It is not, however, a permanent retreat from the world, but only a preliminary move which will enable the soul to see everything in proper perspective and therefore without danger to itself; the promise at the end of *The Preparative* is "so thou shalt even all Admire".

The whole of *The Vision* is a meditation on the attainment of a "view" of Felicity. After the initial "Flight" has been achieved, the soul finds that "The Sight [of Felicity] / Is Deep and Infinit", for it is "all that Ey can see" in "the Godheads Dwelling Place", presumably everywhere. Thus no distinction is here made between spiritual and material things, but the list of objects to be admired is a significantly abstract one—"Glory, Love, Light, Space, / Joy Beauty and Varietie". Traherne believes that earthly things as well as heavenly things can be seen with the eye of the soul, and that man's "sight" of God Himself is not limited to the apprehension of things of the spirit. Indeed, "vision" is a power which can transform even the evil in the external world into a spiritual benefit to the beholder:

> Even Trades them selvs seen in Celestial Light,
> And Cares and Sins and Woes are Bright.

After this general introduction, Traherne delves more

---

2. *Ibid.*, p. 41.
3. Ll. 59–60. Traherne's interpretation of the Sixth Beatitude: "Blessed are the pure in heart: for they shall see God" (Matthew 5 : 8).

deeply into his subject. Most people, he thinks, can see individual beauty in the numerous objects around them, but they do not possess "Blessedness" because they are "Blind" to the "Caus of Bliss" and feel merely overwhelmed by the meaninglessness of these "Ten thousand Heaps of vain confused Treasure". He concludes, therefore, that true "sight" is really a spiritual understanding of "The very Life and Form and Caus of Pleasure", a grasping of the total pattern of Felicity, an ability to "see", as Traherne himself does, that "all things [are] Gods Treasures in their Proper places".[4] Most mystics discover that "Order the Beauty even of Beauty is", but this "Order" cannot be "seen" without the exercise of spiritual discipline; thus the third stanza of *The Vision* summarizes the method by which this end may be reached.

Since the world is a "Spacious Case" enclosing God's beautiful treasures and glorious blessings, neither God nor nature can be understood in isolation from each other. The core of Traherne's advice to his soul is contained in the lines

> For then behold the World as thine, and well
> Upon the Object Dwell.

One must develop a full appreciation of the universe in relation to oneself as the possessor of it by the Creator's plan. Such an altering of perspective will enable one to discern "Order" in everything, to "see" everything in a clearer light. To press his point further, Traherne devotes the whole of the following stanza to an amplification of the last two lines of the first stanza. He illustrates how the misery of others can be turned into one's own joy, their ignorance into one's own knowledge, and their faults into one's own virtues:

> All shall be thine, becaus they all Conspire,
> To feed and make thy Glory higher.

Many readers find this stanza distasteful; nevertheless, it is an integral part of Traherne's thought, and can be compared with lines 44 and 45 of "Mankind is sick":

> The dismal Woes wherein they crawl, enhance
> The Peace of our Inheritance,

and with these sentences in *Centuries* I, 48: "Hell it self is a Part

---

4. *Centuries* III, 60.

of GODs Kingdom, to wit His Prison. It is fitly mentioned in the Enjoyment of the World: And is it self by the Happy Enjoyed, as a Part of the world."

The last three stanzas of this poem are an attempt to describe more fully the experience of "beholding" Felicity. To discover one's own central position in the total pattern (and, by implication, the central position of each person), one's spiritual possession of and lordship over every other creature, is "To see a Glorious Fountain [or Cause] and an End [or Effect]"—God as Power or Father, and God as Love or Holy Spirit in one's own soul.[5] Happiness is attained through an understanding of God's power and love in relation to oneself and as evidenced by His creatures:

> To see all these unite at once in Thee
> Is to behold Felicitie.

In the sixth stanza Traherne abandons his didactic use of the second person singular and returns to the tone of stanzas 1 and 2. Quiet, deep meditation on the blessedness of "seeing" "the King / Of Glory face to face" and on the wonder of comprehending different but united aspects of the mysterious nature of God leads to the poet's ecstatic expression of his own mystical experience, and intense feeling makes the seventh stanza both the natural climax of *The Vision* and a fitting transition to the next poem in the Dobell Folio Manuscript, *The Rapture*. "From One, to One, in one to see *All Things*" is to "see" himself as the "friend" of "the King of Kings" and even, in a sense, as "the End / Of all his Labors", for man is the quintessence of the universe. The realization of his own exalted position is an essential part of Traherne's enjoyment of Felicity:

> Who all things finds conjoynd in Him alone,
> Sees and Enjoys the Holy one.

One of the most striking features of *The Vision* is that in it Traherne makes little distinction between "seeing" material things, "seeing" the things he believes, and "seeing" God;[6] but it is significant that he substitutes the words "understand"

---

5. Traherne discusses the aspects of God as Producer, Means, and End in *Centuries* II, 46.

6. In statements of "seeing" the Divine, Traherne is more daring than most mystics; nevertheless he admits in *Amendment* that God is

and "Comprehend" for "see" in lines 12 and 45. Physical sight is traditionally used as a symbol for the intellective powers of the mind or the soul, and in this respect Traherne follows convention. Even his mystical vision of God involves the spiritual understanding of the unity of all things in God (l. 49) and in himself (ll. 39–40, 55–56).

Closely related to the intellective side of a mystical experience is the conative side. Since mysticism is "the expression of the innate tendency of the human spirit towards complete harmony with the transcendental order",[7] the mystic feels impelled to adjust himself to the greater Reality which he has contacted and, in some measure at least, comprehended. His sense of harmony with that Reality and its purposes is often symbolized by physical hearing.

Traherne makes only general references to "hearing" the "voice" of God giving him information or instruction concerning spiritual matters; for example, he maintains that in childhood he was "Instructed . . . by the Deitie", for

> He in our Childhood with us walks,
> And with our Thoughts Mysteriously he talks,[8]

and that this gift of communication has now been restored: "With God himself I talk."[9] Moreover, he believes that the ear of the soul hears the voices of material objects as well as the direct voice of God:

> evry Thing that I did see,
> Did with me talk,[10]

and that physical sounds can also be heard spiritually: the bells

---

> A DEITIE,
> That wilt for evermore Exceed the End
> Of all that Creatures Wit can comprehend,

and he begins an early poem with the lines

> For Man to Act as if his Soul did see
> The very Brightness of Eternity,

thus implying that men on earth cannot see this "Brightness".

7. Evelyn Underhill, *Mysticism: A Study in the Nature and Development of Man's Spiritual Consciousness* (12th ed. rev.; London, 1930), p. xiv.
8. *The Approach*, ll. 42, 7–8.
9. *Hosanna*, l. 34.
10. *Wonder*, ll. 7–8.

> ev'ry way
> Speak to us throu the Sky:
> Their iron Tongues
> Do utter Songs,
> And shall our stony Hearts make no Reply![11]

Sometimes it is his own soul that is "heard":

> There is som ANGEL that within Me can
> Both Talk and Move.[12]

However, harmony with the world and with oneself is dependent on harmony with God. In the anguish and fear of spiritual alienation Traherne cried to the objects of nature around him,

> Will ye not speak
> What 'tis I want, nor Silence break?[13]

and since "Felicity . . . / Was out of View", he was so eager for "news" of "the Unknown Good" that any "News from a forrein Country" was "wont to call [his] Soul into [his] Ear".[14]

The mystic's sense of cosmic harmony is often expressed in terms of music. Carlyle says, "See deep enough, and you see musically; the heart of Nature *being* everywhere music, if you can only reach it";[15] and Evelyn Underhill claims that "of all the arts music alone shares with great mystical literature the power of waking in us a response to the life-movement of the universe".[16] Traherne is "seeing musically" when he understands with his whole being that "Order the Beauty even of Beauty is",[17] and he seems to have loved music very deeply. More of his images are derived from it than from any other art, and he declares,

> There's no such sacred Joy or solemn Mirth,
> To pleas and satisfy my Heart's Desire,
> As that wherwith my Lord is in a Quire,
> In holy Hymns by warbling Voices prais'd,
> With Eys lift up, and joint Affections rais'd.[18]

---

11. *Bells*, ll. 18–22.
12. *An Hymne upon St Bartholomews Day*, ll. 14–15.
13. *Solitude*, ll. 45–46.
14. *On News*, ll. 33–34, 1–8.
15. "The Hero As Poet", in E. D. Jones (ed.), *English Critical Essays: Nineteenth Century* (London, 1916), p. 261.
16. *Mysticism*, p. 76.
17. *The Vision*, l. 9.
18. *Churches* I, ll. 8–12.

Although Traherne does speak of "hearing" "the Musick of [God's] Works",[19] he more often uses the terms of music to express his sense of complete inner harmony. His soul produces joyful spiritual music which is "heard" by God and by himself:

To see, Approve, take Pleasure, and rejoyce,
Within, is better than an Empty Voice:
No Melody in Words can Equal that;[20]

moreover, all the faculties of his body are together capable of producing heavenly harmony:

Thy Gifts O God alone Ile prize,
My Tongue, my Eys,
My cheeks, my Lips, my Ears, my Hands, my Feet,
Their Harmony is far more Sweet;
Their Beauty true. And these in all my Ways
Shall Themes becom, and Organs of thy Praise.[21]

Most of his music images are inspired by the church music of organ and choir, and this is appropriate not only because the poems are religious, but also because organ-playing and choir-singing alike demand a blending or harmonizing of different voices or parts. The Christian who is in harmony with God, the world, and himself should also be in harmony with other people, and especially with other Christians; thus Traherne speaks of the music which the Church, united in spirit, can make for the ear of the soul. The tongues of those bound by brotherly love are "A Quire of Blessed and Harmonious Songs",[22] for true Christians should "Tunably ring" like a set of church bells:

Being round
And smooth and whole, no Splinters are
In them, no Cracks, nor holes, nor flaws
That may let out the Spirits thence
Too soon; *that* would harsh jarring caus
And lose their Influence.[23]

Traherne's sense of harmony with nature is strengthened by the common belief of his day that from the stars flows an

---

19. *The Estate*, ll. 21–22.
20. *Silence*, ll. 29–31.
21. *The Person*, ll. 59–64.
22. *Goodnesse*, ll. 65–66.
23. *Bells*, ll. 32, 69–74.

ethereal fluid which affects the characters and actions of people. He feels the immediacy of the contact between himself and the stars, the spiritual touch of their influence:

> The very Heavens in their Sacred Worth,
> At once serv us, and set his Glory forth.
> Their Influences touch the Gratefull Sence.[24]

He is also conscious that the stars "shed" "On all things their Nocturnal Influence",[25] and that this fluid or power is "Derivd and borrowed" from God, Who is immanent in "all things";[26] thus he "feels" the "touch" of God, the simple and direct sense of His presence, not only through the "touch" of the stars, but also through the physical touch of material objects:

> Herbs and Flowers aspire
> To touch and make our feet Divine.[27]

In contrast to the more intellectual faculties of sight and hearing, touch is used primarily as an emotional symbol; for a sense of the immediate immanence of God gives above all a pleasing feeling of certitude. Thus Traherne speaks of the stars "Sweetly Shedding" their influence "to [his] pleased Sence", or "saluting" his "pleased Sence" with their influence.[28] But vision and harmony and the certitude of God's presence can all contribute to the mystic's state of blessedness, the purely delectable side of his experience; and the conventional symbols for spiritual satisfactions and rejoicings are the physical senses of taste and smell.[29] However, Mary Anita Ewer points out that these symbols are very seldom used by Christian mystics, partly because the attainment of joy does not demand symbolism and partly because of their prejudices:

> among Occidental peoples there is an insidious conviction that the physical delights of palate and of nostril are somehow unworthy of humanity . . . both joy and the senses

---

24. *Thoughts* IV, ll. 61–63.
25. *Nature*, ll. 61–62.
26. *Goodnesse*, ll. 53–54.
27. *The Estate*, ll. 66–67.
28. *Nature*, ll. 61–62; *Goodnesse*, ll. 53–54.
29. E.g., "O taste and see that the Lord is good" (Psalm 34 : 8), and "I am full, having received . . . the things which were sent from you, an odour of a sweet smell" (Philippians 4 : 18).

which minister rather to joy than to knowledge, are somewhat suspect among us.[30]

It is all the more striking, then, that Traherne does not hesitate to use taste and smell frequently as mystical symbols for his exuberant happiness and enjoyment. This is appropriate to his "Christian Epicureanism"[31] (as he himself described his philosophy)—the pursuit of God, Who is his "Felicity".

With remarkable consistency Traherne gives a special meaning to his symbolism of the chemical senses. The joys of the spiritual tasting or smelling of heavenly or earthly things are nearly always associated in his mind with the inward appreciation of the function of the object which is "tasted" or "smelt". The cherubim were believed to excel in knowledge, yet he calls spiritual taste "a Cherub's Sense" in his statement that Adam

> had a Tongue, yea more, a Cherub's Sense
> To feel its [the world's] Worth and Excellence.[32]

The poet also maintains that David

> ruled by a Law
> That then the Hony Comb
> Was Sweeter far,

and that

> evry Drop that from his flowing Quill
> Came down, did all the World with Nectar fill.[33]

Thus, for him, the intellectual senses of the soul must understand the functional beauty of a thing before its delectable quality can be properly "tasted" or "smelt". The full significance of Traherne's symbolic use of the chemical senses is most clearly stated in his poem, *The Odour*.

In some respects *The Odour* is a companion poem to *The Vision*. Traherne states that

> Who all things finds conjoynd in Him alone,
> Sees and Enjoys the Holy one;[34]

30. Ewer, *op. cit.*, pp. 51–52.
31. Gladys I. Wade, *Thomas Traherne: A Critical Biography* (Princeton, 1944), p. 144.
32. *Adam*, ll. 29–30.
33. "In Salem dwelt a Glorious King", ll. 33–35, 49–50. To David, "the judgments of the Lord" were "sweeter . . . than honey and the honeycomb" (Psalm 19 : 9–10).
34. *The Vision*, ll. 55–56.

and just as *The Vision* is a meditation on "seeing" or comprehending, so *The Odour* is a meditation on "smelling" or enjoying. The comprehension of Felicity begins with the comprehension of the relationship between oneself and the world;[35] similarly, the enjoyment of Felicity begins with the enjoyment of this relationship, and particularly with a deep appreciation of the value to oneself of one's body, since no other part of the material world is "so near". Addressing the members of his own body, Traherne asks:

> If first I learn not what's *Your* Price
> Which are alive, and are to me so near;
> How shall I all the Joys of Paradise,
> Which are so Great and Dear,
> Esteem?[36]

It is noteworthy, however, that in *The Odour* Traherne makes no attempt to specify "the Joys of Paradise"; nor does he explicitly mention the enjoyment of Felicity, "the Holy one", perhaps because enjoyment is here so closely associated with spiritual odour. It seems that Traherne, despite his fondness for using taste and smell symbolically, shares a little of the prejudice of other Christian mystics. In his poems, he does speak of the "Delicious Stream" of the "Nectar" of God's love which

> on Earth . . . doth flow,
> Like Myrrh or Incense even here below,[37]

but he does not refer directly to "tasting" or "smelling" God.

The Odour begins in a mood of rapturous wonder as the poet contemplates various parts of his body. The miraculous thing about them all is that they "Are us'd, yet never waste"; thus there is a very definite connection between Traherne's joy and his realization of the way in which all the parts function. They give their uses continuously for his benefit, yet remain unchanged to the eye, just as fragrant flowers give their perfume:

> My Members all do yield a sweet Perfume;
> They minister Delight, yet not consume.

Function is for him a spiritual odour, and to impress his symbolic

---

35. "For then behold the World as thine" (*The Vision*, l. 17).
36. *The Odour*, ll. 37–41.
37. *Love*, l. 1; *The Enquirie*, ll. 29–30.

meaning on the mind of his reader he addresses the members of his body (stanzas 2–7), restating the idea in different ways; for example,

> Your Uses flow while ye abide:
> The Services which I from you receiv
> Like sweet Infusions throu me daily glide.

In the first four stanzas of the poem there is much emphasis on "sweetness", which is the most common of all traditional symbols for happy spiritual experience.

In the fifth stanza Traherne dedicates his joy in the "*Services*" which "flow" from his body by recognizing the "boundless Lov" of God, the Giver of such "Treasure". He also makes taste, as well as odour, a symbol for function:

> Your Substance is the Tree on which it grows;
> Your Uses are the Oil that from it flows.

The mingling of the two chemical senses is inevitable, and the symbolic meaning of taste, which has already been hinted at in lines 2 and 13, is further demonstrated in stanza 6:

> Thus Hony flows from Rocks of Stone;
> Thus Oil from Wood; thus Cider, Milk, and Wine,
> From Trees and Flesh; thus Corn from Earth; to one
> That's hev'nly and divine.

Similar imagery is found in other poems by this mystic, notably in *The Estate* (ll. 23–27):

> Each Toe, each Finger framed by thy Skill,
> Ought Oyntments to Distill.
> Ambrosia, Nectar, Wine should flow
> From evry Joynt I owe,
> Or Things more Rich;

and here, too, the images are spiritualized by their context, so that "le vin, l'huile, le miel ont la transparence et la généralité des symboles plutôt que la densité de la sensation".[38]

Life is for Traherne the pursuit of the "Highest Bliss",[39] but he maintains in *The Odour* that if one is to enjoy all gifts, even

---

38. Robert Ellrodt, *L'inspiration personnelle et l'esprit du temps chez les poètes métaphysiques anglais*, première partie, II (Paris, 1960), 324.
39. *The Author to the Critical Peruser*, l. 10.

those "at distance", one must first cultivate the spiritual "Sense" to "learn" the "Price" of one's own body, for "By *that* alone thou feelest all the Pleasure"; thus stanzas 8, 9, and 10 (like stanzas 3, 4, and 5 of *The Vision*) contain instruction addressed by the poet to himself. "Liv to thy Self; thy Limbs esteem," he advises, and then offers reasons for this esteem in the form of praises of the body, even declaring that his limbs "are such Works as God himself beseem". The olfactory imagery cannot be fully appreciated if the symbolic meaning of odour has not been grasped. It is his spiritual rejoicing in the functions of the parts of the human body that moves him to write lines such as

> Like Amber fair thy Fingers grow;
> With fragrant Hony-sucks thy Head is crown'd

and

> Where ere thou movest there, the Scent I find
> Of fragrant Myrrh and Aloes left behind.

But in the final stanza of *The Odour* the poet turns abruptly from his comparisons between uses and perfumes, realizing how inadequate they have been to express the true "sweetness" of "sacred *Uses*", a spiritual odour which is indeed ineffable. Even the fragrance of myrrh and aloes is of relatively little beauty if considered apart from its "sacred *Uses*", for physically

> To see, taste, smell, observ; is to no End,
> If I *the Use* of each don't apprehend.

Thus Traherne points emphatically to the symbolic nature of his comparisons between sensory and spiritual experience.

This survey of the poet's sense symbolism reveals that Traherne does distinguish broadly between different senses in a way conventional in mystical writing: "sight" is related to understanding, "hearing" to conation, "touch" to immediacy of contact, and "taste" and "smell" to joy. Nevertheless it also reveals something of the essential originality of his use of these symbols, an originality which springs from unconventional attitudes. Perhaps the most striking feature of his symbolism is its lack of clear distinctions between the spiritual, intellectual, and physical realms. Traherne implies that one can see the outer world, intellectual concepts, and God Himself, all with the eye of the soul, that is, in a spiritual way. With the ear of the soul one can hear the voices of God, of material objects, of physical sounds, and of one's own soul, as well as the harmonious music of nature, of one's own soul or body, and of the Christian family. In a spiritual way one can feel the touch of the stars and the physical touch of material objects, and can taste and smell the outer world, intellectual concepts (such as David's law), God's love, and one's own body. Thus the reader of Traherne's poetry finds traditional mystical symbols used not only for the sensuous expression of the spiritual, but also for the "spiritual" expression of the intellectual and the sensuous. The use of earthly symbols to represent heavenly things—an inevitable ingredient of mystical writing—often becomes rather the use of earthly symbols to represent a spiritualized concept of earthly things; for example, the odour of an object represents its function.

Poems like *The Odour* "testify to a powerful and inspiring coenaesthesia which was a source of such deep and almost uninterrupted delight that it joined the natural man to the spiritual man",[40] and Traherne sometimes treats the physical senses as completely indistinguishable from the spiritual senses:

My Senses were Informers to my Heart,
The Conduits of his Glory Power and Art.
. . . .
. . . . evry Sence
Was in me like to som Intelligence.[41]

The poet's exaltation of the senses is an essential part of his exaltation of man, whom he likes to compare favourably with purely spiritual beings. Indeed, some of his bold statements seem to show a preference for man: "A Dimmer Light / Perhaps would make them [the angels] erre as well as We",[42] and

So greatly high our humane Bodies are,
That Angels scarcely may with these compare.[43]

The rhymed passage beginning "Then shall each Limb a spring of Joy be found"[44] is a demonstration of God's power to make

---

40. H. M. Margoliouth (ed.), *Thomas Traherne: Centuries, Poems, and Thanksgivings* (2 vols.; Oxford, 1958), II, 373.
41. *Nature*, ll. 7–8, 11–12. One is reminded of Blake's belief that "Man has no Body distinct from his Soul; for that call'd Body is a portion of Soul discern'd by the five Senses, the chief inlets of Soul in this age" (from "The Voice of the Devil" in *The Marriage of Heaven and Hell*).
42. "For Man to Act", ll. 20–21.
43. "While I, O Lord, exalted by thy hand", *Thanksgivings for the Body*, ll. 329–30.
44. *Ibid.*, ll. 430–65.

the body a spiritual advantage to man rather than a disadvantage to him.

Since this passage is intended as a description of the resurrected and glorified body of man and the joy of such a transfiguration, when "ev'ry Member" will be "crown'd" "with its Glory", the poet begins in the future tense; but by the fifth line the present tense has already appeared. This makes the future vivid to the reader's mind and enhances the visionary quality of the verse; however, it is significant that it is "all the Senses" which,

> fill'd with all the Good
> That ever Ages in them understood,
> Transported are

—a claim which Traherne would probably not consider too great for man's physical senses in his earthly state. After this parenthesis he reverts to the future tense for a few lines to state that after the resurrection, joy will

> Affect the Soul, though in the Body grow.
> Return again, and make the Body shine
> Like Jesus Christ, while both in one combine.

This leads to an attempt to explain, in seventeenth-century physiological terms, that there are "Mysterious Contacts" "between the Soul" and "its Bowl", the body. Here the present tense seems to broaden the significance of the verse to include earthly as well as heavenly existence, and the future tense is abandoned for the remaining lines of this rhymed passage.

Nevertheless, at this point Traherne is still aware of his post-resurrection meaning expressed by the present tense, so in order to refer plainly to the possibilities of man's earthly life he changes to the past tense for contrast. God is

> He that could bring the Heavens thro the Eye,
> And make the World within the Fancy lie;

thus, in heaven, He

> Far more than this in framing Bliss can do,
> Inflame the Body and the Spirit too:
> Can make the Soul by Sense to feel and see,
> And with her Joy the Senses wrap'd to be.

However, the poet here depicts man's future glorification as very similar to his own experience expressed in *Nature*:

The very Day my Spirit did inspire,
The Worlds fair Beauty set my Soul on fire;

moreover, he says of David that "Sence did his Soul with
Heavenly Life inspire".[45] Traherne evidently believes that on
earth man can attain to the same kind of blessed state as he will
enjoy after the resurrection of the body—a state in which soul
and body are completely inseparable. God has

found the way himself to dwell within,
As if even Flesh were nigh to him of kin,

and the body can therefore "shine" with a spiritual light compared with which the sun is "earthly Darkness".[46] But quite
apart from soul or mind, man's physical nature of itself exalts
him to the highest place in creation; it is

More blessed and divine,
To live and see, than like the Sun to shine.[47]

It is highly characteristic of this mystic that he should so
associate living with seeing, for a study of his sense symbolism
reveals not only a lack of clear distinctions between the spiritual,
intellectual, and physical realms, but also a constant assumption
of the primary importance of sight, which he closely relates to
all the other senses. Traherne links hearing with sight by declaring that

Philosopher and Poet too
Did in his [David's] Melodie appear,[48]

touch with sight in his statement,

A Thought my Soul may Omnipresent be.
For all it toucheth which a Thought can see,[49]

and taste and smell with sight in the lines,

We long to make them see
The sweetness of Felicity.[50]

---

45. "In Salem dwelt a Glorious King", l. 59.
46. "Then shall each Limb a spring of Joy be found", *Thanksgivings for the Body*, ll. 458–59, 461–62.
47. "While I, O Lord, exalted by thy hand", *ibid.*, ll. 325–26.
48. "In Salem dwelt a Glorious King", ll. 45–46.
49. *Thoughts* III, ll. 75–76.
50. "Mankind is sick", ll. 71–72.

Indeed, he sometimes implies that "sight" is the only truly spiritual sense. He maintains that in his "unbodied" early infancy he "forgot" all his physical senses and "was all Sight, or Ey",[51] for

> No Ear,
> But Eys them selvs were all the Hearers there.
> And evry Stone, and Evry Star a Tongue,
> And evry Gale of Wind a Curious Song.[52]

This close association of sight with other senses may be partly explained by the fact that Traherne was a mystic who "found his most powerful organic sensibility in sight, but [whose] other senses were also powerful".[53] Many mystical poems contain vivid complexes of sense images which do not spring from a confusion of ideas, for in moments of ecstasy the senses run into one another and are transcended, and this effect is conveyed by the mingling of images which appeal to different senses. Thus in the opening lines of Shelley's lyric "My soul is an enchanted boat"[54] there is a synaesthetic complex of music-water-motion-colour:

> My soul is an enchanted boat,
> Which, like a sleeping swan, doth float
> Upon the silver waves of thy sweet singing.

Synaesthesia is but the heightening of a normal activity of the human mind—the involuntary linking of different sense impressions so that there seems to be a correspondence between, for example, a certain visual quality and a certain taste, as in the evocative opening of *The Odour*, though here the correspondence is between spiritual rather than physical senses:

> These Hands are Jewels to the Ey,
> Like Wine, or Oil, or Hony, to the Taste.

However, Traherne's emphasis on sight has far deeper causes than these, for lines like "The fair Ideas of all Things"[55] show how greatly he is influenced by Platonism, a system of thought which is the reaction of the intellectualist upon mystical

---

51. *The Preparative*, ll. 31–37.
52. *Dumnesse*, ll. 59–62.
53. Margoliouth, *loc. cit.*
54. *Prometheus Unbound* II, v, 72–110.
55. *The Preparative*, l. 25.

truth. It is Traherne's passionate intellectuality which attracts him to the Platonic and Neo-Platonic philosophers[56] and leads him often to identify soul with mind.[57] Since sight, the "highest" of the senses, is traditionally used as an intellectual symbol, its superiority over the other senses would be most keenly felt by intellectual mystics. Traherne celebrates all the senses, but his doctrine of spiritual possession is founded on the miracle of sight.

To claim, in *Nature*, that "evry Sence / Was in [him] like to som Intelligence" is to declare that there is a relationship of hearing, touch, taste, and smell to sight, and that all the senses can contribute to understanding. One explanation of the poet's fondness for symbolism of the chemical senses is that he makes no real distinction between mystical knowledge and joy, believing that "if you know your self, or God, or the World, you must of Necessity Enjoy it", since "A Sight of Happiness is Happiness".[58] Thus light is used as a secondary symbol for function and is identified with odour in such lines as

> Ye solid are, and yet do Light dispence;
> Abide the same, tho yield an Influence.[59]

The poet also states that function is "taste" and "odour" only "to one / That's hev'nly and divine", adding in explanation:

> He that cannot like an Angel see,
> In Heven its self shall dwell in Misery.[60]

Traherne knows that in the spiritual sphere hearing is sight so deep that it draws the mystic into harmony with God and His purposes; touch is sight so intimate that it assures the mystic of God's presence; and either taste or smell is sight so delectable that it elevates the mystic to a state of blessedness in which he truly possesses Felicity. Since all the "senses" help man to "see" more clearly, "sight" may be regarded as the spiritual faculty which includes all the other "senses", making "Eys them selvs . . . the Hearers"[61] and the human eye an apt symbol for the human soul, whose chief duty is to "see" its "Great *Felicity*" and "enjoy" its "Highest Bliss".[62]

---

56. E.g., *Centuries* IV, 75, 76, and 77 is all from Pico.
57. As in *The Author to the Critical Peruser*, ll. 41, 55.
58. *Centuries* I, 16 and III, 60.
59. *The Odour*, ll. 17–18.
60. *Ibid.*, ll. 33–34, 35–36.
61. *Dumnesse*, l. 60.
62. *The Author to the Critical Peruser*, ll. 7–10.

c

In *The Vision* Traherne outlines the method of attaining "Felicitie", "the Holy one", through an understanding of His power as "Fountain" or Father and His love or goodness as "End" or Holy Spirit. However, he realizes that his picture of Felicity is here unfinished, because in *The Improvment*, the second poem following *The Vision* in the Dobell Folio Manuscript, he states:

> We cannot think the World to be the Throne,
> Of God, unless his *Wisdom* shine as Brother
> Unto his *Power*.

Furthermore, God's wisdom as Means or Son[63] "more doth shine" in "recollecting" than in creating, and God "recollects" His creation by receiving "the Sacrifice of *Endless Prais*" from man, the only creature capable of the spiritual appreciation of His works by "seeing" the central position (paradoxically) of each man in the "*Marvellous Designe*" of "that Great *Architect*". Thus it is the eye of man which makes it possible for God to "recollect" His creation and which therefore bears constant witness to His wisdom (stanza 4):

> But neither Goodness, Wisdom, Power, nor Love,
> Nor Happiness it self in things could be,
> Did not they all *in one fair Order* move,
> And joyntly by their Service End in *me*.
> > Had he not made an *Ey* to be the Sphere
> > Of all Things, none of these would e're appear.

Sometimes Traherne emphasizes the symbolic meaning of the eye by sharply contrasting his physical eyes with his spiritual eye, as in the poem *Sight*:

> Two Luminaries in my Flesh
> > Did me refresh;
> But one did lurk within,
> > Beneath my Skin,
> *That* was of greater Worth than both the other;

for

---

63. Traherne discusses the aspects of God as Producer, Means, and End in *Centuries* II, 46.

> This Ey alone,
> (That peer hath none)
> Is such, that it can pry
> Into the End
> To which things tend,
> And all the Depths descry
> That God and Nature do include.

More often, however, the distinction between physical and spiritual is blurred, and this can lead to an apparent confusion of ideas, as in the second section of the poem *Innocence*.

Here Traherne maintains that his soul "Did . . . flie / All Objects that do feed the [physical] Eye", while it loved "those very Objects" "Which in their Glory most are hid" because of their commonness. "Their Constant Daily Presence" "which takes them from the Ey / Of others" was seen and enjoyed by Traherne. This is consistent with his assertion in *The Demonstration* that

> Be it a Sand, an Acorn, or a Bean,
> It must be clothd with Endless Glory,
> Before its perfect Story
> (Be the Spirit ne're so Clear)
> Can in its Causes and its Ends appear.

But why does the poet say that his appreciation of the common "Objects" around him took place when

> A Serious Meditation did employ
> My Soul within, which taken up with Joy
> Did seem no Outward thing to note?

The word "seem" (l. 15) is very important, because Traherne's theory of knowledge does not clearly distinguish between image and concept, and in all his *Thoughts* poems there are lines like the following:

> What were the Skie,
> What were the Sun, or Stars, did ye [Thoughts] not lie
> In me! and represent them there
> Where els they never could appear![64]

"Ce qu'il admire le plus, c'est que notre simple faculté de per-

---

64. *Thoughts* I, ll. 43–46.

ception transporte [le monde sensible] en l'âme",[65] for his keen awareness of the inner presence of the representations of all things in his mind is the foundation for his conviction that all is his. Traherne's "Serious Meditation" is partly the exercise of forming pictures of glorious outward objects in his mind or soul, and "Their Constant Daily Presence" which "offerd them" to him is primarily an inner presence of material things. But even though the second section of *Innocence* is based on "the representation of . . . sensory experience . . . in imagination",[66] sight, as used in this section, may still be regarded as a symbol for a spiritual faculty, because the poet clearly indicates that he is referring to an experience which is not merely intellectual or sensory. In the poem *On News* there is greater emphasis on the spiritual possession of "all the Treasures of the World" by means of the soul's faculty of sight. His "Glorious Soul" "Made to possess them" was, he says,

> The Heavenly Ey,
> Much Wider then the Skie,
> Wher in they all included were.

Traherne uses the eye symbol most impressively when he attempts to describe experiences which are beyond the range of those which more ordinary persons may enjoy. At times the mystic is completely unaware of himself as a physical creature and feels wholly existent in the inner core of his spiritual being, which ceases to be complex and becomes a unity of "Simple Sence", "A Naked Simple Pure *Intelligence*":

> Then was my Soul my only All to me,
> A Living Endless Ey,
> Far wider then the Skie
> Whose Power, whose Act, whose Essence was to see.[67]

Traherne's fullest expression of this kind of spiritual sense experience is *My Spirit*,[68] which in the Dobell Folio Manuscript is directly followed by *The Apprehension*, a fragment in which he admits that such an experience can be momentary only, but claims that the intellectual "Apprehension" of the experience "serves its purpose at times when the vision is absent":[69]

---

65. Ellrodt, *op. cit.*, première partie, II, 303.
66. Ewer, *op. cit.*, p. 35.
67. *The Preparative*, ll. 39, 20, 11–14.
68. This poem is examined on pp. 129–32.
69. Margoliouth, *op. cit.*, II, 351.

> If this I did not evry moment see,
>   And if my Thoughts did stray
>   At any time, or idly play,
>   And fix on other Objects, yet
>   This Apprehension set
>   In me
>   Was all my whole felicitie.

There is no doubt, however, that the poet regards man as most like God and therefore closest to Him when he becomes "A Living Endless Ey", because in some of his poems the eye symbolizes God.

Mystics often speak of God's spiritual senses as well as of their own. Thus Traherne boldly claims that

> Our Blessedness to see
> Is even to the Deitie
> A Beatifick Vision![70]

for

> all his Happiness doth seem,
> . . . .
> In that Delight and Joy to lie
> Which is his Blessed Creatures Melodie.[71]

God, he says, most desires "Gratitude, Thanksgiving, Prais,/ A Heart returnd"; therefore

> These are the Nectar and the Quintessence
> The Cream and Flower that most affect his Sence.[72]

Since all the "senses" are to Traherne different aspects of the highest one, "sight", it is logical that he should use the eye as a symbol for God as well as for the soul of man.

The spherical shape of the physical eye is another reason for its appropriateness as a symbol for any spiritual being, for the seventeenth century was peculiarly conscious of the circle as a symbol for the absolute perfection of Infinity and Eternity.[73]

---

70. *The Recovery*, ll. 7–9.
71. *The Demonstration*, ll. 67–70.
72. *The Recovery*, ll. 55–56, 59–60.
73. E.g., one of Vaughan's most inspired openings, the beginning of *The World*, depends largely on the circle symbol for its effectiveness:

> I saw Eternity the other night
> Like a great *Ring* of pure and endless light . . .

In the poem *On News*, Traherne calls his "Glorious Soul" not only a "Heavenly Ey" but also

> The Ring Enclosing all
> That Stood upon this Earthy Ball,

and in *The Preparative* he declares:

> I was an Inward *Sphere of Light*,
> Or an Interminable Orb of *Sight*.

This imagery is similar to that used in the poem *Felicity* to refer to God, for according to this mystic, "the Mind of God, that Sphere of Lov",

> is all full of Sight,
> All Soul and Life, an Ey most bright,
> All Light and Lov.

Thus the poet clearly links the highest kind of "Sight" with the circle of Infinity and Eternity.[74]

Traherne asks,

> What is there which a Man may see
> Beyond the Spheres?

and his answer is "FELICITY", one of his names for God.[75] Moreover, he maintains that in achieving the goal of his "vision", man becomes, like God, "an Interminable Orb of *Sight*". This is Traherne's way of asserting that man is exalted to the state of divinity in the act of fulfilling his passion for the Infinite.

---

74. Cf. Henry More's description of the soul's condition in moments of ecstasy: "She is one orb of sense, all eye, all airy ear" (*Prae-existency of the Soul*, stanza 102, l. 9).

75. *Felicity*, ll. 7–9.

II

LIGHT

BEING INFINITELY PRESENT IN EVERY PLACE, THOU MAKEST ME
PERCEPTIVE, AND I SEE THY GLORY.
(TRAHERNE: *Thanksgivings for God's Attributes*)

TRAHERNE CLOSELY ASSOCIATES LIGHT WITH ALL HIS SPIRITUAL
experiences, as do most mystics. When spirit and body are
felt to be inseparable and God makes "the Soul by Sense
to feel and see",

> His Goodness, Wisdom, Power, Love divine,
> Make, by the Soul convey'd, the Body shine.[1]

When the "living spirit absorbs and surpasses the physical senses"
so that "the distinction between body and spirit disappears",[2]
man becomes

> an Inward *Sphere of Light*,
> Or an Interminable Orb of *Sight*

irradiating all the objects of his perception:

> Tis not the Object, but the Light
> That maketh Heaven; Tis a Purer Sight.[3]

Illumination of the world within and without is the mystical
experience which Traherne most clearly shows in his poetry.

"To 'see God in nature', to attain a radiant consciousness
of the 'otherness' of natural things, is the simplest and commonest
form of illumination";[4] but so constant and overpowering is

---

1. "Then shall each Limb a spring of Joy be found", *Thanksgivings for the Body*,
ll. 450, 460–61.
2. K. W. Salter, *Thomas Traherne: Mystic and Poet* (London, 1964), p. 66.
3. *The Preparative*, ll. 15–16, 57–58.
4. Evelyn Underhill, *Mysticism: A Study in the Nature and Development of Man's
Spiritual Consciousness* (12th ed. rev.; London, 1930), p. 234.

Traherne's apprehension of the Infinite Life immanent in external objects that he claims the universe as God's Body of Manifestation.[5] His sense of a unity in separateness and his vision of an added significance and reality in the phenomenal world are the results of an enhanced mental lucidity which is accompanied by an abnormal sharpening of the senses. Hence, for this mystic, the gulf between the worlds of spirit and sense no longer exists:

> His Glory Endless is and doth Surround
> And fill all Worlds, without or End or Bound.
> What hinders then, but we in heav'n may be
> Even here on Earth did we but rightly see?[6]

He perceives in physical experiences themselves a revelation and interpretation of spiritual reality; the ringing of church bells prompts him to exclaim,

> If Lifeless Earth
> Can make such Mirth,
> What then shall Souls abov the starry Sphere![7]

All objects, he feels, have an ultimate sanctity and divine significance:

> In all Things, all Things service do to all:
> And thus a Sand is Endless, though most small.
> And every Thing is truly Infinite,
> In its Relation deep and exquisite.[8]

This mystical perception forms the basis for Traherne's symbolic comparisons between physical and spiritual powers.

God is traditionally defined as Light, and mystics realize that no misconception of the Divine is possible in conceiving of overwhelming Light. In the desolation of alienation from God Traherne cries, "Will nothing to my Soul som Light convey!",[9] but when he finds Felicity, "Whose Strength and Brightness so do

---

5. *Centuries* II, 20, 21.
6. *Thoughts* IV, ll. 33–36.
7. *Bells*, ll. 9–11.
8. "As in a Clock", ll. 29–32. One is reminded of the famous opening lines of Blake's *Auguries of Innocence*:

> To see a World in a Grain of Sand
> And a Heaven in a Wild Flower,
> Hold Infinity in the palm of your hand
> And Eternity in an hour.

9. *Dissatisfaction*, l. 8.

Ray, / That still it seemeth to Surround",[10] he sees Truth shining on all and the earth "Encircled in a Sphere of Light" and appearing like a star.[11] Since this illuminated vision of the world is granted only to those who "rightly see", spiritual light is closely related to the eye of the soul, the light by which all things (including itself) are seen.[12] The eye may therefore be regarded as one of the many mystical symbols of light.

Traherne claims that evil "Fled from the Splendor of [his] Eys"[13] and that

> Those Things that are most Bright
> Sun-like appear in their own Light;[14]

but the mystic knows that God is the ultimate Light by which all spiritual truth becomes visible and by which He Himself is seen:

> Eternity it self is that true Light,
> That doth enclose us being infinite.[15]

If God is "an Ey most bright",[16] how much more is He like "The reall Sun, *that* hev'nly Ey",[17] for

> God is Himself the Means,
> Wherby he doth exist:
> And as the Sun by Shining's clothd with Beams,
> So from Himself to All His Glory Streams,
> Who is a Sun, yet what Himself doth list.[18]

Christian sun symbolism has its roots in ancient pagan fertility rites, as the choice of the date for Christmas reveals. The Winter Solstice was regarded as the annual birth-date and

---

10. *Innocence*, ll. 43–44.
11. *The Designe*, l. 40; *Adam*, l. 36; *Admiration*, l. 13.
12. *The Preparative*, ll. 15–16, 57–58.
13. *Wonder*, l. 52.
14. *The Demonstration*, ll. 23–24.
15. *Thoughts* IV, ll. 41–42.
16. *Felicity*, l. 20.
17. *Dreams*, l. 5.
18. *The Anticipation*, ll. 50–54. It is interesting to note that Traherne is sometimes aware of the possible inadequacy of the sun symbol, as is shown by ll. 65–68 of *The Circulation*:

> The Moon returneth Light, and som men say
> The very Sun no Ray
> Nor Influence could hav, did it
> No forrein Aids, no food admit.

dawn as the diurnal birth-time of the Sun-God, the divine Servant of humanity, Giver of life (power), light (wisdom), and heat (love), whom death takes, but over whom death has no dominion; and all of these ideas are implicit in the poem *On Christmas-Day*. The bells rang "At break of Day" to welcome Christ, Who "Makes Winter, Spring". By His death He serves man, for " 'Tis He that Life and Spirit doth infuse":

> Ev'n thou, O King,
> As in the Spring,
> Dost warm us with thy fires
> Of Lov: Thy Blood hath bought us new Desires
> Thy Righteousness doth cloath with new Attires.

This symbolism is hallowed by a long tradition. Both David and Isaiah refer to God as a Sun,[19] and Malachi (4 : 2) specifically calls the promised Messiah "the Sun of righteousness". The darkening of the sun at Christ's crucifixion[20] lends weight to the already-established symbol, and St. John pictures the New Jerusalem as a city filled with the light of the uncreated Sun.[21] Thus in Traherne's childhood vision of a city called Christendom, the sun's "Heat and Light" seemed "shed" on everything "With such a dazling Lustre" "As made [him] think 'twas th' *New Jerusalem*".[22] Its three great gifts of life, light, and heat make the sun a particularly apt symbol for the Christian God, Whose chief attributes of Power, Wisdom or Truth, and Love or Goodness are sometimes thought of as corresponding to the Persons of the Trinity—Father, Son, and Holy Spirit. Traherne often refers not only to the Sun's Light but also to His Life and Heat; for example, in *The Anticipation* he describes "the Fountain Means and End" as

> a Glorious Bright and Living Flame,
> That on all things doth shine,
> And makes their Face Divine.

Although Traherne's joy in the physical sun leads him to write of it most often in a literal way, his words are tinged with an awareness of its symbolical associations. Thus he says that "The

---

19. Psalm 84 : 11 and Isaiah 60 : 20.
20. Luke 23 : 45.
21. "And the city had no need of the sun . . . to shine in it: for the glory of God did lighten it, and the Lamb is the light thereof" (Revelation 21 : 23).
22. *Christendom*, ll. 66–70.

Burning Sun doth shew [God's] Love" and that "The Glorious Sun the Knowing Soul enflames".[23] Even his statement in *Right Apprehension* that the sun is "more Glorious than a Costly Throne" bears an implicit reference to the King of Kings. Indeed, so spiritual is his vision of the material world that it is at times impossible to separate the literal from the symbolical, as when he declares that on earth "a Fire / Not scorching but refreshing glows",[24] or that

> The Soft and Swelling Grapes that on their Vines
> Receiv the Lively Warmth that Shines
> Upon them, ripen there for me.[25]

Since "His Nature burns like fire",[26] God can refine the "common Ore" of the believer's soul into "Mettal pure" which, like a church bell, is fit to praise Him on high and capable of drawing other souls up to Him:

> From Clay, and Mire, and Dirt, my Soul,
> From vile and common Ore,
> Thou must ascend . . . .
> . . . . ;
> Refin'd by fire, thou shalt a Bell
> Of Prais becom, in Mettal pure;
>
> . . . .
>
> Refin'd by Lov,
> Thou still *abov*
> Like them [bells] must dwell, and other Souls allure.[27]

This traditional kind of transmutation symbolism would strengthen the poet's concept of God as the Sun of his soul, for in the seventeenth century mines were considered to be produced by the sun's heat. Traherne maintains in *The Dialogue* that the sun "Concocteth Mines" and in *The Estate* that

> The Sun it self doth in its Glory Shine,
> And Gold and Silver out of very Mire,
> And Pearls and Rubies out of Earth refine.

---

23. *The Rapture*, l. 15; *Thoughts* IV, l. 60.
24. *The World*, ll. 20–21.
25. *Goodnesse*, ll. 49–51.
26. *The Anticipation*, l. 93.
27. *Bells*, ll. 34–36, 38–39, 42–44.

Similarly, man can be enriched by a close relationship with God only when his soul has been purified by receiving the warming beams of Love which overcome his baser nature. Sometimes man's soul is pictured not as ore to be refined by God's Love but as a portion of the Divine Fire itself. The man who is "Drown'd" in worldly customs is dead to natural beauty and to the life of the spirit, for he has become

> A Stranger to the Shining Skies,
>   Lost as a dying Flame;[28]

but he who, like David, craves for inward perfection becomes "A Constant Heavenly Pure Seraphick Flame",[29] excelling in love as the seraphim were believed to do. Thus the transmutation of base metal into the spiritual gold of God's nature is equivalent to the transformation of a "dying Flame" into a "Constant . . . Flame", and this identification of gold with fire is really a form of sun symbolism. Traherne poetically relates material gold to the physical sun, as when he expresses his amazement at the fact that men "rejoyce in a Piece of Gold more then in the Sun";[30] and in the language of the Hermetic philosophy, so popular among mystical writers of the seventeenth century, "Sol" means "spiritual gold".[31]

Behind the use of alchemical symbols there is always the assumption that it is possible for man to partake fully of the nature of God Himself. With Traherne, as with most mystics, the illuminated vision of the world, which forms the basis for such comparisons as that between the sun and God, is accompanied by an illumination of the self—a joyous and overwhelming sense of the presence of God within his own soul. This perception of the splendour of the world within is naturally expressed by the symbolism of light, for man's kinship with God is keenly felt by one who experiences a flooding of the personality with spiritual radiance. However, Traherne's originality subtly shines through his seemingly traditional descriptions of the light in man's soul. Since Traherne was conversant with the work of the Cambridge Platonist Henry More,[32] it is useful to compare and contrast

---

28. *The Apostacy*, ll. 60–62.
29. "In Salem dwelt a Glorious King", l. 78.
30. *Centuries* I, 34.
31. Cf. Vaughan, "The unthrift Sunne shot vitall gold / A thousand peeces" (*Regeneration*, ll. 41–42).
32. C. L. Marks, "Thomas Traherne and Cambridge Platonism", *PMLA*, LXXXI (1966), 521 (2), 529–30.

stanzas 101 and 102 of More's *Prae-existency of the Soul* with a
passage in Traherne's poem, *Nature*.

To illustrate his doctrine of illumination, More borrows
and adapts an allegory from Cornelius Agrippa:

> Like to a light fast-lock'd in lanthorn dark,
>
> . . . .
> Some weaker rays through the black top do glide,
> And flusher streams, perhaps, from horny side.
> But when we've pass'd the peril of the way,
> Arriv'd at home, and laid that case aside,
> The naked light how clearly it doth ray,
> And spread its joyful beams as bright as summer's day.
>
> E'en so the soul in this contracted state,
> Confin'd to these strait instruments of sense,
> More dull and narrowly doth operate.
>
> . . . .
> . . . . But when she's gone from hence,
> Like naked lamp she is one shining sphere,
> And round about has perfect cognoscence
> Whate'er in her horizon doth appear.
> She is one orb of sense, all eye, all airy ear.[33]

Traherne's description of one of his ecstatic experiences has
obvious similarities:

> My Inclinations raisd me up on high,
> And guided me to all Infinitie.
> A Secret self I had enclosd within,
> That was not bounded with my Clothes or Skin,
> Or terminated with my Sight, the Sphere
> Of which was bounded with the Heavens here:
> But that did rather, like the Subtile Light,
> Securd from rough and raging Storms by Night,
> Break through the Lanthorns sides, and freely ray
> Dispersing and Dilating evry Way:
> Whose Steddy Beams too Subtile for the Wind,
> Are such, that we their Bounds can scarcely find.
> It did encompass, and possess rare Things,
> But yet felt more, and on its Angels Wings

---

33. Quoted by Percy H. Osmond in *The Mystical Poets of the English Church*
(London and New York, 1919), pp. 208–9.

Pierc'd through the Skies immediatly, and sought
For all that could even any where be thought.
It did not move, nor one way go, but stood,
And by Dilating of it self, all Good
It strove to see, as if twere present there,
Even while it present stood conversing here:
And more suggested then I could discern,
Or ever since by any Means could learn.

Both poets emphasize the unity of being which the human soul can achieve by becoming "one shining sphere", the superiority of spiritual knowledge over other kinds of knowledge, and the brightness and strength of the soul's light. But Traherne makes bolder claims for man than More does in this particular passage. He stresses the soul's insatiable urge to "encompass, and possess rare Things", its seeking "For all that could even any where be thought"—a seeking which can, moreover, be successful:

My Inclinations raisd me up on high,
And guided me to all Infinitie.

His soul is not content to have "perfect cognoscence / Whate'er in her horizon doth appear"; instead, its "Steddy Beams" which "freely ray / Dispersing and Dilating evry Way" "Are such, that we their Bounds can scarcely find". Furthermore, Traherne does not altogether discard the body in favour of the soul, even though he admits its limitations. To More, the soul is "a light fastlock'd" in the "lanthorn dark" of the body, which must be "laid . . . aside"; to Traherne, the "Secret self" is so forceful and demanding that it can "Break through the Lanthorns sides" and make the physical senses its servants, "The Conduits of [God's] Glory Power and Art".[34]

This reaching out of his soul "to all Infinitie" and this sense of its unlimited possibilities impel Traherne "to this very conclusion which the conscious doctrinal mind is reluctant to make, that this secret self, this 'sphere of Light' is also God".[35] Though he evades explicitly stating this belief, it is often implicit in the imagery and symbolism which he employs in an attempt to express his experiences. Thus in *The Preparative* he describes his soul not only as "A Living Endless Ey" but also as

---

34. *Nature*, l. 8.
35. Salter, *op. cit.*, p. 69.

> An Endless and a Living Day,
> *A vital Sun* that round about did *ray*
> All Life and Sence

—a description which most Christians would reserve for God alone. Even where the word "sun" is not mentioned, there are many suggestions of sun symbolism which refer to his own soul. In *My Spirit* the poet says that his spirit "Strongly Shind/ Upon the Earth, the Sea, the Skie", and in *Hosanna* he compares his thoughts with "vital Beams" because

> They reach to, shine on, quicken Things, and make
> Them truly Usefull; while I *All* partake.

That Traherne is here implying a comparison with the physical sun becomes clearer after reading the list of activities which he attributes to it in *The Dialogue*; for example, he says that the sun "Concocteth Mines", "Doth quicken Beasts, revive thy vital Powers", and "animats the Trees". Indeed, so daring is he in his use of the sun symbol that he compares even the human body with the sun, using terms which are usually applied to spiritual life only. The following passage from *The Estate* shows how inseparable the worlds of spirit and sense seem at times to Traherne:

> Mens Bodies were not made for Stripes,
>   Nor any thing but Joys.
> They were not made to be alone:
>   But made to be the very Throne
> Of Blessedness, to be like Suns, whose Raies,
> Dispersed, Scatter many thousand Ways.[36]

Such imagery may have arisen partly from the mystic's association of light with the functions of the human body, as in *The Odour*: "Ye [members] solid are, and yet do Light dispence."

As most people would agree that man is on a higher level of creation than the physical sun, the full implication of the poet's sun imagery can be felt only by the reader who is familiar with the traditional uses of symbols. Admittedly, man is occasionally compared favourably with the sun in mystical writing because of his gifts of soul and mind; for example, Vaughan speaks of

---

36. Ll. 31–36. It is perhaps significant that Philip Traherne, more cautious and orthodox than Thomas, omitted from his version the stanza in which this passage appears.

> The way which from this dead and dark abode
> Leads up to God,
> A way where you might tread the Sun, and be
> More bright than he.[37]

The forceful last line of the poem *Sight*, in which Traherne maintains that "no Light in Hev'n more clearly shines" than the eye of his own soul, is therefore perfectly acceptable to the most orthodox of believers if the word "Hev'n" is here taken to mean "the sky"; and so is his reference in "Then shall each Limb a spring of Joy be found" to the sun as "earthly Darkness" as compared with the shining of a body which "subject lies / To those Affections which in Souls arise",[38] since this rhymed passage deals specifically with a state of being in which soul and body are indistinguishable from each other. But as a mystic aware of and sensitive to the symbolical associations of natural phenomena, Traherne is unusual in that he sometimes contemplates the superiority of man's body over that sun which gives him so much pleasure. In the passage beginning "While I, O Lord, exalted by thy hand", he presents an elevated picture of the human body, and then exclaims:

> Suns are but Servants! Skies beneath their [bodies'] feet;
> The Stars but Stones; Moons but to serve them meet;[39]

furthermore, in *Admiration*, a poem devoted to a portrayal of all creation, including angels and cherubim, adoring the divinity of the "Human Shape", the poet mentions that the sun may

> Be overcom
> With Beams that shew
> More bright than his,

and reaches a climax in the last stanza, where he depicts the sun's joy in serving man, "A Creature so divine", "one that livs / Abov himself". The poem ends in a tone of rapturous wonder:

> Lord! What is Man that he
> Is thus admired like a Deity!

It is interesting to contrast the light symbolism of Vaughan

---

37. *The World*, ll. 53–56.
38. *Thanksgivings for the Body*, ll. 461–62, 452–53.
39. *Ibid.*, ll. 335–36.

and Traherne, two mystical poets of the same period who see God as both transcendent and immanent. Vaughan, apprehending Reality with an emphasis on the transcendence of the Godhead, is oppressed by a feeling of God's inaccessibility and by a sense of loss. All created forms, he believes, contain the star-fire of spirit, and in *Cock-crowing* he expresses the idea that man contains a "Sunnie seed" of light which should be much stronger than that "glance of day" in the cock. But the immortal soul is partially obscured by the mortal veil of flesh; it is a star "confin'd into a Tomb", unable to "shine through all the sphære" till it is "resumed" from "this world of thrall".[40] Thus he pleads with God to take off this veil or cloud:

> O take it off! make no delay,
> But brush me with thy light, that I
> May shine unto a perfect day,
> And warme me at thy glorious Eye![41]

The noontide brilliance of Traherne's imagery is very different from the chiaroscuro luminosity of Vaughan's. Traherne, apprehending Reality with an emphasis on the immanence of the Godhead, and uplifted by a feeling of God's presence and by a sense of well-being, sees the fire of the human spirit as more akin to the sun than to a star. Thus he believes that on earth the "Sunnie seed" is free to become "*A vital Sun*", and the "glance of day" to become "An Endless and a Living Day".[42] Instead of being thought of as an imprisoning "Tomb", a mere hindrance to spiritual development, the body is enjoyed by Traherne as one of God's greatest gifts. His use of the veil symbol therefore takes on a different significance.

Traherne does not deny that there is a veil which partially hides God from man, but he implies that this veil need not necessarily be a serious or a permanent restraint to communion with Him in this life. References in his poems to God's inaccessibility are not only rare and vague, but are also related to man's ability to appreciate nature; in *Eden* he maintains that in childhood

> No briers choakt up my Path, nor hid the face
> Of Bliss and Beauty, nor Ecclypst the Place.

---

40. "They are all gone into the world of light!", ll. 29–36.
41. *Cock-crowing*, ll. 44–46.
42. *The Preparative*, ll. 17–18.

D

The veil between this world and the next seems transparent to a mystic who loves this life so much that he feels already in Heaven, for "To hav Blessings and to Prize them is to be in Heaven".[43] Traherne is far more concerned with the eternal present than with the past or the future, but when he does speak of life after death, as in the poem *Shadows in the Water*, he stresses the clarity of his vision of the future, and the thinness of the "Skin" separating the two worlds:

> I plainly saw by these [reflections]
> A new *Antipodes*,
> Whom, tho they were so plainly seen,
> A Film kept off that stood between.
>
> . . . .
> . . . . below the purling Stream
> Som unknown Joys there be
> Laid up in Store for me;
> To which I shall, when that thin Skin
> Is broken, be admitted in.

By contrast, Vaughan "looks before and after", and uses characteristically the language of exile from "the world of light".

In his use of the veil symbol Traherne tends to elevate this world to a position which is usually occupied by Heaven in the writings of Christian mystics. Since the illuminated vision of the world is possible only for those who "purely see", he refers to the veil of sin and error which can hide earthly beauty from the eyes of man. He insists in *The Apostacy* that in early infancy

> No Mud did foul my limpid Streams,
> No Mist eclypst my Sun with frowns;
> Set off with hev'nly Beams,
> My Joys were Meadows, Fields, and Towns,

and in *Eden* that

> No Error, no Distraction I
> Saw soil the Earth, or overcloud the Skie.

These fairly general references to sin are given an original flavour if the reader is aware that in the opinion of this poet, the gravest error of all, and that which most surely separates man from God, is the false valuation of the works of men's hands above the

---

43. *Centuries* I, 47.

glories of the creation in which God reveals Himself, glories which Traherne habitually includes among his spiritual "Treasures". Thus, as in the poem *Hosanna*, the obscuring veil is sometimes identified with "Wealth new-invented":

> No more, No more shall Clouds eclyps my Treasures,
> Nor viler Shades obscure my highest Pleasures;
>> No more shall earthen Husks confine
>> My Blessings which do shine
> *Within* the Skies, or els *abov*:
>
> . . . .
>> . . . . . . Heven here
>> Would be, were those remov'd;
>>> The Sons of Men
>>> Liv in Jerusalem,
>>> Had they not Baubles lov'd.
> These Clouds dispers'd, the Hevens clear I see.

Like most mystics, Traherne speaks of the "Dull Walls of Clay"[44] which are a potential danger to the human spirit within; but he places his emphasis not on the power of sin or on the limitations of earthly existence but on the miraculous power of the spirit to shine unhindered through the flimsy veil of flesh:

> What Powerfull Spirit livs within!
> What Active Angel doth inhabit here!
>> What Heavenly Light inspires my Skin;
> Which doth so like a DIETIE appear![45]

His frequent mentions of skin, which testify to a powerful sense of touch,[46] are not derogatory. Rather is he fascinated by the mystery of

> A Spiritual World Standing within,
>> An Univers enclosd in Skin,[47]

by the paradox of human beings—"Inward Cherubins"—being "cloath'd with mortal Skin".[48] Traherne insists that the offending veil is not the body so much as "Wealth new-invented" which

---

44. *An Hymne upon St Bartholomews Day*, l. 19.
45. *Ibid.*, ll. 1–4.
46. H. M. Margoliouth (ed.), *Thomas Traherne: Centuries, Poems, and Thanksgivings* (2 vols.; Oxford, 1958), II, 373.
47. *Fullnesse*, ll. 7–8.
48. *The Bible*, ll. 8–9.

blinds men's souls to natural beauty; thus in *The Inference* I he laments that

> A Feast, fine Cloaths, or els a Trade,
> Take up their Thoughts; and, like a grosser Skreen
> Drawn o'r their Soul, leav better Things unseen.

The esteem that Traherne feels for the human body is based primarily on his conviction that on earth it can be used as an organ of the soul, just as it will be after the resurrection. The poem *Hosanna* begins as a triumphant hymn of praise to God for his soul's ability to absorb his body instead of being bounded by it:

> No more shall Walls, no more shall Walls confine
> That glorious Soul which in my Flesh doth shine:
> No more shall Walls of Clay or Mud
> Nor Ceilings made of Wood,
> Nor Crystal Windows, bound my Sight,
> But rather shall admit Delight.

Nevertheless, like Blake, he also feels delight in the body for its own sake, a delight which springs from interest in its perfect mechanism and from artistic admiration of the nude. In many poems he celebrates the glories of the human form, and in *The Person* clearly states his preference for the unveiled body and for the unveiled description of it:

> The Naked Things
> Are most Sublime, and Brightest shew,
> When they alone are seen:
> . . . .
> Their Worth they then do best reveal,
> When we all Metaphores remove,
> For Metaphores conceal,
> And only Vapours prove.
> They best are Blazond when we see
> The Anatomie,
> Survey the Skin, cut up the Flesh, the Veins
> Unfold: The Glory there remains.
> The Muscles, Fibres, Arteries and Bones
> Are better far then Crowns and precious Stones.

It is natural that a mystic original enough in his thinking to compare men's bodies with "Suns, whose Raies, / Dispersed,

Scatter many thousand Ways"[49] should associate the veil symbol
with the body's light as well as with the light of the spirit; and in
both *The Person* and *The Author to the Critical Peruser* there is also
an association between naked man and "naked Truth" uncon-
cealed by metaphorical "Vapours". Thus Traherne indirectly
declares a kinship not only between God and the soul, but also
between God and the body, for both soul and body partake of
the Light of Truth.

That man is made in the image of God is a theological
platitude which Traherne is particularly fond of expressing. He
says that one of his chief reasons for accepting the Bible as a
Book from Heaven is that "There I was told / That I *the Son
of God* was made, / *His Image*",[50] and he believes that good
thoughts "bear the Image of their father's face".[51] Indeed in
his short poem *The Image* he proclaims,

> If I be like my God, my King,
> (Tho not a Cherubim,)
>   I will not care,
> Since all my Pow'rs derived are
> From none but Him.

It is therefore natural that he should make use of the Platonic
symbol of the mirror. He describes his soul in the course of a
deep spiritual experience as "The Mirror of an Endless Life",[52]
for the soul which clearly reflects God has reached the highest
state to which it may rise. Thus in *Thoughts* IV he prays,

> O give me Grace to see thy face, and be
> A constant Mirror of Eternitie.

If the soul is a mirror reflecting God Himself, it must also
reflect spiritual qualities which man can share with God. In the
poem *Sight* Traherne pictures the eye of his soul as

> A Looking-Glass
> Of signal Worth; wherin,
>   More than mine Eys
>   Could see or prize,
> Such things as Virtues win,
> Life, Joy, Lov, Peace, appear'd.

---

49. *The Estate*, ll. 35–36.
50. *The Bible*, ll. 1–3.
51. *Thoughts* III, l. 31.
52. *Fullnesse*, l. 5.

However, as he explains in *The Preparative*, the soul can be "inflamed" by "Divine Impressions" only when it has been cleansed of all impurities and "thus prepard for all Felicity":

> Pure Empty Powers that did nothing loath,
> > Did like the fairest Glass,
> > Or Spotless polisht Brass,
> Themselvs soon in their Objects Image cloath.

It is significant that Traherne's inclination toward the immanent rather than the transcendent God leads him to think of the soul as a mirror of the whole material creation also, just as objects are mirrored in the physical eyes of man; and in *Amendment* he shows clearly that "Divine Impressions" need not be limited to purely spiritual things. The poem is based on the idea that God delights in His creatures far more when men appreciate them and offer up thanks for them than when He first created them; they "far more Brightly shine" in the mirror of the human soul than in themselves, for God, being Pure Spirit, does not share man's need of material things, though He is within them. Traherne, overwhelmed by amazement at the importance of man's position in the universe and at the great honour which God has bestowed on man, asks in wonder:

> And is my Soul a Mirror that must Shine
> Even like the Sun, and be far more Divine?

Paradoxically, the images of things that dwell in man "do all Substances Excell".[53]

Traherne's psychological curiosity finds expression in his many poems praising the power of human thought, an important proof to him that man is indeed a divine image of God. One of his recurring themes is that by thoughts man can transcend the bounds of time and place:

> By you I do the Joys possess
> Of Yesterdays-yet-present Blessedness;
> > As in a Mirror Clear,
> > Old Objects I
> Far distant do even now descrie
> Which by your help are present here.[54]

---

53. "Ye hidden Nectars, which my GOD doth drink", l. 7.
54. *Thoughts* I, ll. 13–18.

On a much higher plane, God also transcends the bounds of time and place; and this conviction of the likeness between Creator and man leads Traherne to describe God in a similar way. He is the One

> Whose Bosom is the Glass,
> Wherin we all Things Everlasting See.
> His Name is NOW, his Nature is forever.[55]

Despite the obvious association of "Eye" with "Glass", this is a rather unexpected use of the mirror symbol, a symbol very closely related to the created image rather than to the great Original Himself. It reminds the reader of the fact that thoughts of the deification of man—a traditional theme of Hermetic philosophy and Renaissance humanism—sometimes carry Traherne to the brink of heresy, as when he declares in *The Recovery* that God places "his Whole Felicitie" in man's enjoyment of and gratitude for the created world, and that He is "despised and defied / Undeified almost if once denied".

It is an inflated picture of man that Traherne paints in his poems. He describes the eyes of the body in the traditional way as "Those living Stars",[56]

> Those Eys of Sense
> That did dispense
> Their Beams to nat'ral things;[57]

but in his vision so closely does man mirror God that the eye of the soul "which throu the Hevens went"[58] is, in its highest moments, not merely a spiritual star, a seed of light, but "*A vital Sun*" free to "Break through the Lanthorns sides" of the body, which can itself be compared with the sun. This exalted picture is the product of the personal experience of a mystic whose soul reached out "to all Infinitie".

---

55. *The Anticipation*, ll. 24–26.
56. *The Preparative*, l. 3.
57. *Sight*, ll. 13–15.
58. *Ibid.*, l. 19.

III

WATER

... THE SOUL IS A MIRACULOUS ABYSS OF INFINIT ABYSSES, AN UNDRAINABLE OCEAN, AN INEXHAUSTED FOUNTAIN OF ENDLES OCEANS, WHEN IT WILL EXERT IT SELF TO FILL AND FATHOM [GOD'S TREASURES].
(TRAHERNE: *Centuries* II, 83)

WATER SYMBOLS, LIKE LIGHT SYMBOLS, ARISE FROM AN apprehension of the Deity immanent in external objects and in oneself. To the illuminated vision of the mystic the sun is a great source of life, light, and heat which manifests God's Power, Wisdom, and Love; similarly, a fountain is a source of life and water which manifests in particular His regenerating Power and His purifying Love. Thus in Traherne's poems there is often a mingling of sun and fountain imagery, whether the meaning is symbolic or not. In *Right Apprehension* the poet describes the sun's "warming Beam" as

> A living Stream
> Of liquid Pearl, that from a Spring
> Waters the Earth,

and in *Nature* he says that the "fountain of Delights" which "must needs be Lov" "shines upon [him] from the highest Skies". When he speaks of the sun's "Floods of Light",[1] the reader is reminded that even in common expressions like "flood-light" there is an association of light with water. Nevertheless, Traherne seems to be aware of the partial inadequacy of the fountain symbol to represent the Trinity unless it is combined with light imagery, for God's Wisdom or Truth is usually symbolized by light.

In versified theological discussions such as *The Anticipation*, God the Father, the all-powerful and life-giving Creator, is

---

1. *The World*, l. 69.

constantly referred to as "the Fountain" as distinct from "the Means" or God the Son, and from "the End" or God the Holy Spirit, and the great mystery of Three in One and One in Three is expressed in statements like "The End and Fountain differ but in Name", and

> God is Himself the Means,
> Wherby he doth exist.[2]

One could hardly claim that such a poem contains fountain imagery, since the reader is given no picture of water pouring forth. "Fountain" is here a symbol which is not brought to life by the poet, and which remains merely a convenient name for the Father. But whenever Traherne gives vitality to this symbol for God, his mind turns to the living waters of Divine Love streaming freely from the Fountain of Eternal Life. In the poem *Love*, the thought of God as "The fountain Head of evry Thing" leads to the ecstatic wonder of the third stanza:

> Did my Ambition ever Dream
> Of such a Lord, of such a Love! Did I
> Expect so Sweet a Stream
> As this at any time!

Significantly, Traherne never in his poems uses water symbols to refer specifically to God's wisdom, for which the light-giving sun is a more appropriate symbol. Thus, when speaking of God's attributes in *The Enquirie*, he states that "His Wisdom Shines, on Earth his Lov doth flow".

Since Traherne's vision of the material world is essentially a spiritual one, he sometimes pictures all of God's creatures, and especially the great and common blessings such as the stars and the sun, flowing forth from the Creator or "Fountain" as concrete symbols of His love for man:

> As Living Waters from his Throne they trill.
> As Tokens of his Lov they all flow down.[3]

He sees earthly streams of water as "True Living Wealth" which "At once my Body fed, and Soul did Crown",[4] for God, Who is to be enjoyed in everything, is constantly preserving man's physical and spiritual life, even if

---

2. *The Anticipation*, ll. 36, 50–51.
3. *Thoughts* IV, ll. 68–69.
4. *Speed*, ll. 7, 12.

We cold and Careless are, and scarcely think
Upon the Glorious Spring wherat we Drink.[5]

Traherne expresses his consciousness of communion with God and of dependence upon Him for spiritual nourishment by his use of food and drink symbols, most of which are clearly related to the fountain symbol. In the poem beginning "Mankind is sick", he speaks of

The life and splendour of Felicity,
Whose floods so overflowing be,
The streams of Joy which round about his Throne,
Enrich and fill each Holy One,

and in *Thoughts* IV he prays:

Let my pure Soul . . . .

. . . .
Spend all its Time in feeding on thy Lov.

This feeling of sharing the Divine Life is also evident in his claim that God chooses him to "fill, and taste, and give, and Drink the Cup";[6] but unlike Herbert, he seldom refers so specifically to the Christian sacraments, and there is a passage in his poem *Solitude* which may indicate that he sees the potential danger in the beauty of religious ritual:

Th' External Rite,
Altho the face be wondrous sweet and fair,
Will never sate my Appetit
No more than empty Air
Yield solid Food.

Characteristically, Traherne refuses to think of the Creator as apart from His creation. If God is Food and Drink to the believer's soul, so is His world, which can help to fill man's spiritual hunger and thirst. Hence his rather startling but very poetic statements like

The very Seas do overflow and Swim
With Precious Nectars as they flow from him,[7]

and "We plough the very Skies, as well / As Earth".[8] However,

---

5. *Another*, ll. 9–10.
6. *Love*, l. 34.
7. *Thoughts* IV, ll. 43–44.
8. *The Estate*, ll. 57–58.

he often emphasizes that material things can give truly spiritual nourishment only to those souls which have found God and themselves, and that however beautiful nature may be, it is meaningless if considered in isolation from Him and from themselves. Even in the early poem *Memento mori*, Traherne states that

> Not all the Treasures, nor the Pleasures,
>> Where with the Earth is fill'd;
> Can meat afford, fitt for the Board,
>> where Soules are to bee still'd,

and *Solitude* and *Dissatisfaction* are vivid and moving accounts of his desperate attempts to satisfy the raging thirst for "Absent Bliss"[9] that tormented him in his youth. The lovely things around him seemed "sullen" and even terrifying in their indifference towards him; he "pin'd for hunger at a plenteous Board".[10] He rejected the false claims of human knowledge, natural beauty, material wealth, and common pleasures to be the highest sources of true happiness, finding all of them "sensless as Trees" in comparison with the "Book from Heven" for which he yearned.[11] The feverishness of his search is conveyed partly by urgent questions in staccato rhythms:

> My Thirst did burn;
> But where, O whither should my Spirit turn![12]

But in his fine poem *Desire* Traherne looks back on the spiritual agony which he suffered at this period of his life and passionately thanks God for giving him "An Eager Thirst" that "made [his] flesh like Hungry Thirsty Ground", ready to receive the Divine Love and restlessly discontented with anything less.

Christ Himself symbolized the Holy Spirit by the water which satisfies thirst, and both water and heat are traditional and appropriate symbols for the Spirit's cleansing power experienced in the lives of all true believers.[13] Just as the Divine Fire of Love transmutes the soul's base metals into spiritual gold, so the water

---

9. *On News*, l. 38.
10. *Solitude*, ll. 41, 24.
11. *Dissatisfaction*, ll. 57, 73. Traherne has often been compared with Wordsworth, but one could not imagine Wordsworth calling trees "sensless".
12. *Ibid.*, ll. 49–50.
13. John the Baptist said, "I indeed baptize you with water; but . . . he [Christ] shall baptize you with the Holy Ghost and with fire" (Luke 3 : 16).

or blood pouring from the Eternal Fountain refines the soul which drinks it. In *My Spirit*, a poem in which he describes the experience of feeling "nigh of Kin / To God", Traherne declares, "I felt no Dross nor Matter in my Soul, / . . . such as in a Bowl / We see", and in triumphant tones he thus concludes an address to Sin:

> Is not my Savior Dead!
> His Blood, thy Bane; my Balsam, Bliss, Joy, Wine;
> Shall Thee Destroy; Heal, Feed, make me Divine.[14]

Moreover, he has discovered that it is Christ's blood which enables him to gain sustenance from God's works:

> Sin spoil'd them; but my Savior's precious Blood
> Sprinkled I see
> On them to be,
> Making them all both safe and good.[15]

To the eyes of the mystic, nature itself seems transformed by the Passion of Christ.

Traherne's longing for God's love is of a different kind from that of most Christian mystics, and indeed it often seems to be a form of spiritual hunger for an assurance of his own importance in God's scheme. He finds satisfaction for this hunger in the Platonic idea of the circulation of all things from God to man and back to God—a theory which has a very prominent place in his poetry and which he develops with new and far-reaching implications, concentrating always on man's exalted position in the universe. According to Traherne, God "made our Souls to make his Creatures Higher",[16] for man's love of the Creator's works transmutes these material gifts into spiritual gifts and offers them back to Him in a refined form which is more acceptable to a purely spiritual Being. The poet's contemplation of God's goodness in allotting to man such a sacred duty gives rise to rapturous exclamations such as

> O how doth Sacred Lov
> His Gifts refine, Exalt, Improve![17]

and

---

14. *The Recovery, Centuries* III, 50, ll. 9–11. This is a different poem from the one with the same title in the Dobell Folio Manuscript.
15. *The World*, ll. 13–16.
16. *Amendment*, l. 49.
17. *Ibid.*, ll. 43–44.

What more Desirable Object can
Be offerd to the Soul of Hungering Man![18]

Some of his statements of the circulation theory are extremely daring; for example, in *The Demonstration* he maintains that

GOD is the Spring whence Things came forth
Souls are the fountains of their Real Worth.

. . . .

In them he sees, and feels, and Smels, and Lives.

Like many other mystics, Traherne pictures God as thirsting for man's love[19] and as thirsting to save man from sin;[20] but he is unusual in that when he conceives of God as refreshing His thirst, it is not simply with man's love, but with the spiritualized images of the created world which man forms in the mirror of his soul and gives to the Creator in grateful love. In the course of expounding the theory of circulation the poet asks in amazement:

Am I a Glorious Spring
Of Joys and Riches to my King?[21]

Even more explicit is his ecstatic address to his own "Pleasant Thoughts" as "Ye hidden Nectars, which my GOD doth drink, / Ye Heavenly Streams",[22] since it is clear that by "Thoughts" he here means images rather than concepts. The importance that he gives to God's material creation, and especially to the human body, is also revealed in his belief that earthly delights "feed and pleas" the appetites of the angels,[23] who find the "Human Shape" so "taking" that they "com and sip / *Ambrosia* from a Mortal Lip".[24]

The Christian soul is like God in that it thirsts for the salvation of others[25] and is refreshed by their love:

Their rich Affections do like precious Seas
Of Nectar and Ambrosia pleas.[26]

---

18. *The Demonstration*, ll. 35–36.
19. *Another*, stanza 2.
20. "Mankind is sick", ll. 57–61.
21. *Amendment*, ll. 29–30.
22. "Ye hidden Nectars", ll. 11, 1–2.
23. *The Enquirie*, ll. 13–15.
24. *Admiration*, ll. 1–3.
25. "Mankind is sick", ll. 62–63.
26. *Goodnesse*, ll. 61–62.

The soul is also like God in that it provides drink for others, for it overflows continuously with the sweet "streams of Joy" from the Eternal Fountain.[27] These food and drink symbols are here used in a thoroughly traditional way, but Traherne's use of them can be more original. In *Thoughts* I his acknowledgment that God "seated" thoughts or "Heavenly Springs" in his spirit does little to alter the impression created by the tone of the whole poem that the poet tends at times to think of himself as a self-sufficient fountain refreshing his own soul rather than as a humble human being dependent chiefly on God for spiritual nourishment:

> Ye Thoughts and Apprehensions are
> The Heavenly Streams which fill the Soul with rare
> Transcendent Perfect Pleasures.
>
> . . . .
>
> And better Meat
> Ye daily yeeld my Soul to eat,
> Then even the Objects I esteem
> Without my Soul.

There is even a suggestion that the stream of his own thought has power to transmute the qualities of his soul or mind, for some of his words are tinged with alchemical associations:

> It [a thought] is the Substance of my Mind
> Transformd, and with its Objects lind.
> The Quintessence, Elixar, Spirit, Cream.

Traherne's boldest use of the fountain symbol is in the poem *Fullnesse*, where he comes very close to identifying himself with God. It is difficult to realize that in the following lines he is presumably speaking of the state of his own soul during a mystical experience, and of the subsequent importance to him of this experience:

> It is a Fountain or a Spring,
> Refreshing me in evry thing.
> From whence those living Streams I do derive,
> By which my Thirsty Soul is kept alive.

Such statements are the direct outcome of his remarkably strong sense of the power of God within him to deify his own soul so that at times it seems one with Him:

---

27. "Mankind is sick", stanza 8.

Are Men made Gods! And may they see
So Wonderfull a Thing
As GOD in me![28]

As has been implied on page 14 of this study, many mystics express their feeling of the Divine Presence within them in terms of spiritual touch. Even if this feeling is overwhelming, it is at the same time often vague and formless, like the mighty power of an immense ocean flowing through one's inner being, nourishing and regenerating the soul with its life-giving waters. Traherne expresses his sense of spiritual fullness and vitality in the rich imagery of these lines from *Wonder*, one of the loveliest of his songs of joy:

I felt a Vigour in my Sence
That was all SPIRIT. I within did flow
With Seas of Life, like Wine.

Similar water imagery is found in the last stanza of *Desire*; but it is noteworthy that here "The Living Flowing Inward Melting, Bright / And Heavenly Pleasures" are clearly stated to be the God-given powers of his own soul, "Sence, feeling, Taste, Complacency and Sight".

A peculiarity of many mystical experiences is that within and without are one, for while God actually seems to be part of oneself, the self is also swallowed up in Him; the soul is filled with and yet surrounded by light and water. Thus spiritual touch frequently becomes submersion in the Divine Light or in the Divine Ocean, and the individual soul is pictured as a mere drop in the Ocean of Infinity. Traherne makes obvious use of these traditional symbols in *Goodnesse*:

While Millions bathe in Pleasures,
And do behold his Treasures
The Joys of all
On mine do fall
And even my Infinitie doth seem
A Drop without them of a mean Esteem.

These lines may seem completely conventional to the casual reader, but a deeper study is rewarding.

---

28. *Amendment*, ll. 31–33.

The word "Millions" is typical of a poet whose "Inclinations" "guided [him] to all Infinitie"[29] and who could be contented with nothing that was limited or bounded. Even more typical is the rhyming of "Pleasures" and "Treasures", for his obsessive repetition of these words in poem after poem is a constant source of annoyance to readers who do not share his mental engrossment in the connotation of these terms which are so much a part of "Christian Epicureanism". More importantly, though, the "Millions" of other people "bathe" not in God but in the "Pleasures" which He gives, and "behold" not God, but rather "his Treasures". In his poetry Traherne shows a consistent tendency to identify the Giver with His gifts, as when he declares:

> Now in this World I him behold,
> And me enveloped in more then Gold;
> In deep Abysses of Delights,
> In present Hidden Precious Benefits,[30]

and

> I never Glorious Great and Rich am found,
> Am never ravished with Joy,
> Till ye [mental images] my Soul Surround,
> Till ye my Blessedness display.[31]

His Christianity sometimes seems very close indeed to pantheism. Furthermore, in *Goodnesse* the poet says that without "The Joys of all", "even [his own] Infinitie doth seem / A Drop . . . of a mean Esteem". The emphasis on the word "even", however, indicates that perhaps his most treasured joy is the infinity of his own soul, and that he does not usually consider it "of a mean Esteem". This passage seems more remarkable still in the light of tradition, for the ocean and water-drop symbols generally express the disproportion of the Infinite to the finite, whereas Traherne uses them to express the mystery of an Infinity of infinities.

Some of his most interesting uses of the ocean symbol arise from his belief that the whole cosmic movement is circular. Despite the problem of salt and fresh water, the generally accepted opinion in the seventeenth century was that all rivers proceed

---

29. *Nature*, ll. 17–18.
30. *The Approach*, ll. 33–36.
31. "Ye hidden Nectars", ll. 21–24.

from and take their circular way back to the heart of the deep.[32]
The statement in Ecclesiastes (1 : 7) that "unto the place from
whence the rivers come, thither they return again" is repeated
by Traherne in *The Circulation*:

> To Seas, that pour out their Streams
> In Springs, those Streams repair.

The final stanza of this poem applies the circulation theory to
God and man:

> He is the Primitive Eternal Spring
> The Endless Ocean of each Glorious Thing.
> The Soul a Vessel is
> A Spacious Bosom to Contain
> All the fair Treasures of his Bliss
> Which run like Rivers from, into the Main,
> And all it doth receiv returns again.

These lines contain two separate yet overlapping pictures. The
first is of God, "Whose All sufficient Love", with the "Joys and
Glories" which are symbols of this love, circulates continuously
within Himself from the Fountain (Father) to the Ocean (Holy
Spirit) and back again to the Fountain.[33] The second is of the
human soul, a "Spacious Bosom" continuously receiving "All
the fair Treasures of his Bliss" and returning them to the Source.
The implications of this double pattern are hinted at in the line
which states that these "Treasures" "run like Rivers from, into
the Main", for here Traherne seems to use "the Main" as a
symbol for both God and man; Ocean and water-drop are seen
rather as Ocean and ocean. Since the Holy Spirit is the name
Christians give to the activity and presence of God in themselves
and in the world around them, the dual significance of the ocean
symbol may arise partly from the idea that the Holy Spirit is
the End or "the Main". "Lov is the Spirit of GOD. . . In us it is
the H. Ghost."[34]

Traherne's boldest use of this symbol is in the third stanza
of *The Estate*, a stanza omitted in Philip Traherne's version.
After comparing "Mens Bodies" to "Suns", the poet continues:

---

32. Marjorie Hope Nicolson, *The Breaking of the Circle: Studies in the Effect of the
"New Science" upon Seventeenth-Century Poetry* (rev. ed.; New York, 1960), pp. 140–41.
33. Traherne explains these ideas more fully in *Centuries* II, 40–47.
34. *Centuries* II, 45.

> They [bodies] Drink in Nectars, and Disburs again
>   In Purer Beams, those Streams,
>   Those Nectars which are causd by Joys.
>   And as the spacious Main
> Doth all the Rivers, which it Drinks, return,
> Thy Love receivd doth make the Soul to burn.

Here he clearly shows that man's body as well as his soul is involved in the process of transforming God's creatures into spiritual gifts to be returned to the Creator, and he implies that the body too, and not only the soul, is a "spacious Main" which "Drinks" in the "Rivers" of Divine Love, presumably by means of the senses, and returns them to God. As is usual in Traherne's poetry, spiritual taste is symbolically related to function or uses, for while the soul burns in responsive love towards Him, the body demonstrates this love by its holy actions, "Nectars" which are "Purer" in God's esteem than His original gifts. However, in *The Estate*, as in *The Circulation*, he does not insist on the idea that man as well as God is an ocean with nearly as much emphasis as in this passage from *Silence* (ll. 61–74):

> An unperceived Donor gave all Pleasures,
> There nothing was but I, and all my Treasures.
> In that fair World one only was the Friend,
> One Golden Stream, one Spring, one only End.
> There only one did Sacrifice and Sing
> To only one Eternal Heavenly King.
> The Union was so Strait between them two,
> That all was eithers which my Soul could view.
> His Gifts, and my Possessions, both our Treasures;
> He mine, and I the Ocean of his Pleasures.
> He was an Ocean of Delights from Whom
> The Living Springs and Golden Streams did com:
> My Bosom was an Ocean into which
> They all did run. And me they did enrich.

These apparently illogical lines are so characteristic of him that it is important to grasp the implications of his thought and expression in them.

Philip Traherne omitted lines 61 and 62 from his version of *Silence*, probably because his orthodox mind was shocked by the suggestion that during a deeply spiritual experience God was "unperceived" and the poet was aware of nothing but his own self and his "Treasures". It becomes clear, however, that

Traherne means that his consciousness of his own overwhelming joy in the spiritual possession of the beautiful things of nature around him preceded his real perception of God, a particularly deep awareness of the one "Friend" Who was the Source of all his joy. This process of an expansion of vision to include first himself and his "Treasures" and then God the Giver is the basis for the conviction which he expressed in his brother's notebook: "That all things are our Treasure immediately we owe it to the Goodnes of our Nature, but finaly to him from whom we received both it and them."[35]

Traherne's description of the Triune God is similar to that in the final stanza of *The Circulation*, and just how precise his use of traditional symbols can be is shown by his apt use of the adjective "Golden" to describe the "Stream" which represents the Son, "the Wisdom of the Father"[36] usually symbolized by the light-giving sun. But the "End" of the "Spring" and "Stream" is presumably the Ocean of the Holy Spirit and also the ocean of his own soul, since in the preceding lines the poet has stressed that at this time he felt himself to be the sole receiver of God's "Treasures", and near the end of the poem he maintains:

> to Himself in me he always gave,
> All that he takes Delight to see me have.

Accordingly, "One Golden Stream" seems to refer not only to Christ but also to the rich stream of the material creation pouring forth from the "one Spring"; and indeed, so strong is Traherne's apprehension of the immanent Godhead that "One Golden Stream, one Spring" becomes indistinguishable from "The Living Springs and Golden Streams" of God's gifts running into and enriching the ocean of his soul. Even though he speaks intimately of God as his "Friend" and "King", the "Union" between God and the soul is conceived primarily as a sharing of "Possessions" and secondarily as a relationship between persons. This is one of his chief peculiarities as a Christian mystic, as is his emphasis on the possessive enjoyment of the created world which is felt by God and man alike. God is "an Ocean of Delights" surrounding the soul, just as the soul is filled with His gifts and is therefore "the Ocean of his Pleasures".

---

35. Quoted in H. M. Margoliouth (ed.), *Thomas Traherne: Centuries, Poems, and Thanksgivings* (2 vols.; Oxford, 1958), II, 348.
36. *Centuries* II, 43.

The picture of man which Traherne presents by means of traditional water and light symbols differs considerably from the traditional one of a limiting and dark body containing a soul, "that Drop, that Ray / Of the clear Fountain of Eternal Day".[37] He was sure that while communing with God, with external nature, and with himself, his very body was like the "spacious Main" and the sun, and

> A vast and Infinit Capacitie,
> Did make [his] Bosom like the Deitie[38]

—not a mere drop of the "clear Fountain", but itself a regenerating and purifying fountain and ocean; not a mere ray of "Eternal Day", but itself "An Endless and a Living Day".[39] Audacious though the expression of his mysticism may be, Traherne's ardent sincerity saves him from the charge of arrogance, if not from a lack of the particular kind of religious humility that most Christian mystics feel. No reader can doubt the genuineness of his spiritual fervour, least of all in those daring passages in which he tries to convey something of the wonder of his own experience. Perhaps his answer to the charge of pride would echo the words of Peter and John: "we cannot but speak the things which we have seen and heard."[40]

---

37. Marvell, *On a Drop of Dew*, ll. 19–20.
38. *Silence*, ll. 75–76.
39. *The Preparative*, l. 17.
40. Acts 4 : 20.

IV

SPACE

TILL YOUR SPIRIT FILLETH THE WHOLE WORLD, . . . YOU NEVER ENJOY
THE WORLD.

(TRAHERNE: *Centuries* I, 30)

LIKE MOST MYSTICS, TRAHERNE'S CHIEF CONCERN AS A WRITER
is to spread the message of his own enlightenment, and his
vision of the exaltation of man is an integral part of this
message. He believes that he himself and other men are divine
because he feels the presence of God within him and because
there are times when the powers of his own soul seem akin to
those of God, the Infinite One. It is above all his passion for and
attainment of absolute freedom of spirit that convince him of
the divinity of man's soul, for in its

>   concealed Face,
> Which comprehendeth all unbounded Space,
> GOD may be seen.[1]

His childhood vision of Christendom was of a city "Where
Souls might dwell in all Delight and Bliss" without restriction:

>   No Wall, nor Bounds
>   That Town surrounds;
> But as if all its Streets ev'n endless were;
> Without or Gate or Wall it did appear.[2]

Moreover, one of his main convictions is that

> 'Tis Art that hath the late Invention found
>   Of shutting up in little Room
>   Ones boundless Expectations: Men
>   Have in a narrow Penn
> Confin'd themselvs: Free Souls can know no Bound.[3]

---

1. *The Author to the Critical Peruser*, ll. 55–57.
2. *Christendom*, ll. 19, 47–50.
3. *The City*, ll. 51–55.

Freedom from the bondage of sin is one of the great traditional themes of Christianity, but Traherne's treatment of it is as unconventional as some of his ideas about sin. The veil of "Wealth new-invented"[4] which obscures the true riches of God's creation imprisons man by limiting his blessings. For Traherne, to be "as free / As if there were nor Sin, nor Miserie" is to be

> prepard for all Felicity,
> Not prepossest with Dross,
> Nor stifly glued to gross
> And dull Materials that might ruine [him],[5]

> For Golden Chains and Bracelets are
> But Gilded Manicles, wherby
> Old Satan doth ensnare,
> Allure, Bewitch the Ey.[6]

Veil and prison images are often inextricably interwoven in his poetry, for he tends to think of the veil primarily as a bond. In *Nature* he compares his "Secret self" to a "Subtile Light" "That was not bounded with [his] Clothes or Skin", and *Dissatisfaction* begins with the striking lines:

> In Cloaths confin'd, my weary Mind
> Persu'd Felicity.

Traherne's desire for spiritual possession of the visible universe is an aspect of his desire for the freedom of unlimited expansion of the self. Even in the naïve section beginning "In Making Bodies"[7] from his early poem about moderation, his passion for the vast is revealed by the mere fact that he finds it necessary to defend God's wisdom in limiting the size of human bodies. He demonstrates how inconvenient it would be if man were a "Monster" with "every Thumb or Toe a Mountain", and arrives at the comforting conclusion that "GOD made Man Greater while He made Him less", since

> An Understanding that is Infinit,
> . . . .
> Is the most Sacred Greatnes may be viewd.

---

4. *Hosanna*, l. 48.
5. *The Preparative*, ll. 49–50, 41–44.
6. *The Person*, ll. 55–58.
7. *Centuries* III, 19.

In "As in a Clock", a revised section of the same poem about moderation, he uses similar arguments to solve the problem of the limited size of other created things, again emphasizing that true infinity is greater than literal vastness:

> And which is best, in Profit and Delight,
> Though not in Bulk, he made all Infinite.

This passion for the infinite tends to make him dissatisfied with finite symbols to express his religious experiences, and sometimes results in a refreshingly original use of the "pilgrimage" idea.

It is the experience of mystic growth and development that leads to the comparisons in mystical literature between physical and spiritual processes; and while transmutation symbols arise out of the concept of conversion as an internal change and from a longing for inward purity, directional symbols of progress arise out of the concept of conversion as a change in the direction of the life-course and from a "longing to go out from [the] normal world in search of a lost home".[8] Conventional references to the spiritual journey or voyage are, however, very few and general in Traherne's poetry. In *Adam* he states that

> Sin is a Deviation from the Way
> Of God: 'Tis that wherin a Man doth stray
> From the first Path wherin he was to walk,

and in *Misapprehension* that

> Man hath lost the ancient Way,
> That Road is gon into Decay;
> Brambles shut up the Path, and Briars tear
> Those few that pass by there.

In *The Anticipation* he warns himself and his reader thus against the perils of drawing heretical conclusions from the circulation theory: "Such Sands, such Dangerous Rocks we must beware." His early poem beginning "Rise noble soule" deals with the progress of lovers in terms of a steep and difficult ascent together up the "hill of rest" to blissful regions of union, but this appears to be a physical rather than a spiritual love poem—which is perhaps why, in the manuscript, all the stanzas are crossed

---

8. Evelyn Underhill, *Mysticism: A Study in the Nature and Development of Man's Spiritual Consciousness* (12th ed. rev.; London, 1930), p. 126.

through for deletion.[9] Poems such as *Solitude* and *Dissatisfaction* are a curious blend of the literal and the symbolical, for although they are fairly straightforward records of the poet's search for Felicity, they are also based on the symbol of the mystic quest. For example, in *Dissatisfaction* he pictures his mind or spirit as running through every street "to meet / [His] Bliss" and knocking at every door in vain "Until *the Bible* [him] supply'd". However, by far his most fascinating use of the "pilgrimage" idea involves the projection of his imagination into space.

"The Circle of Perfection, from which man for so long deduced his ethics, his aesthetics, and his metaphysics, was broken during the seventeenth century", for the limited Ptolemaic concept of the universe as a neat series of perfect spheres within the outermost circle of the fixed stars was completely shattered by "an old idea that came back with new meaning and apparent proof: *the idea of the infinity of the universe and an infinity of worlds*".[10] Many men felt belittled by the newly-revealed vastness of space and sought refuge in older ideas and attitudes, but daring and insatiable souls like Henry More and Thomas Traherne wholeheartedly welcomed the new discoveries and allowed their thoughts to wander through infinity as well as through eternity. Astounded yet enthralled by infinite space, they passionately exulted in the greatness of man, "whose imagination could expand with the universe, whose soul grew vaster with vastness".[11] According to Traherne, man's spirit by nature aspires to eternity and infinity and cannot rest till it has grasped them, and *Insatiableness* II, with many more of his poems, vividly expresses the avid desire for knowledge and the space-intoxication of "This busy, vast, enquiring Soul":

> It will all see,
> Not Time alone, but ev'n Eternity.
>
> . . . .
>
> 'Tis mean Ambition to desire
> A single World:
> To many I aspire,

9. H. M. Margoliouth (ed.), *Thomas Traherne: Centuries, Poems, and Thanksgivings* (2 vols.; Oxford, 1958), II, 405.

10. Marjorie Hope Nicolson, *The Breaking of the Circle: Studies in the Effect of the "New Science" upon Seventeenth-Century Poetry* (rev. ed.; New York, 1960), pp. 7, 157–58.

11. *Ibid.*, p. 194.

Tho one upon another hurl'd:
Nor will they all, if they be all confin'd,
    Delight my Mind.

. . . .

Each one of all those Worlds must be
Enricht with infinit Variety
    And Worth; or 'twill not do.

Such a soul is not content to depict the mystic quest in the traditional way as a land journey or even as a voyage to Heaven across the ocean of time or of eternity, for the physical ocean is confined within shores, while eternity is unbounded. "Prompted to seek [his] Bliss abov the Skies",[12] Traherne discerns "endless Space" by the aid of his spiritual eye "which throu the Hevens went";[13] it is a spiritual and psychological necessity for him to fulfil his passion for the infinite, and he does so partly through what would now be called his powers of imagination:

My better Sight
Was infinit,
New Regions I must see.
In distant Coasts new Glories I
    Did long to spy.[14]

Thus in his poetry the mystic quest is often represented as the imaginative flight of a free soul through the infinite ocean of space to "behold Eternity", Which Traherne identifies with Infinity and with Bliss:

Till I what was before all Time descry,
The World's Beginning seems but Vanity.
    My Soul doth there long Thoughts extend
        No End
Doth find, or Being comprehend:
        Yet somwhat sees that is
        The obscure shady face
            Of endless Space,
        All Room within; where I
Expect to meet Eternal Bliss.[15]

---

12. *Felicity*, l. 1.
13. *Sight*, ll. 3, 19.
14. *Ibid.*, ll. 28–32.
15. *Insatiableness* I, ll. 3, 21–30.

He maintains in *Nature* that the intuition of infinity granted to him in his youth was the divine spark in his soul that led him to soar into an infinity of universes, elevating to the power of the infinite the principles of plenitude and of variety in them all, and to awake to the presence of the Giver of such magnificent gifts, if not always to a clear apprehension of Him:

> But yet there were new Rooms, and Spaces more,
> Beyond all these, Wide Regions ore and ore,
> And into them my pent-up-Soul like fire
> Did break, Surmounting all I here admire.
> . . . .
> All, all was mine. The fountain tho not Known,
> Yet that there must be one was plainly shewn.

Space is his means of coming closer to comprehension of the true Infinite.

There are, however, more important differences between traditional mystic journeys and Traherne's flights than the fact that he travels through space instead of across land or sea to find God. In their depiction of spiritual progress as a journey, most mystics are conscious and deliberate symbolists; they do not imagine that they are actually crossing land or sea, or believe that such a journey of the imagination would bring them nearer to God. By comparison Traherne's flights are fairly literal, and he clearly believes that the freer his spirit is to roam abroad, the more akin to God he is: "This Sight"

> which doth comprehend
> Eternity, and Time, and Space,
> Is far more dear,
> And far more near
> To him, then all his Glorious Dwelling Place.[16]

So although the poet's imaginative exploration of space in poems such as *Nature* and *Consummation* is to him a kind of pilgrimage to Heaven, his space journeys are not symbolical in any strict sense of the word. Furthermore, they do not picture more or less definite steps or stages in his spiritual life. This may be partly explained by the fact that in Post-Reformation English mysticism, the *Scala Perfectionis* is never insisted on as an indispensable framework of the mystic's progress;[17] but the primary cause lies

---

16. *Thoughts* II, ll. 37–42.
17. W. K. Fleming, *Mysticism in Christianity* (London, 1913), p. 179.

in the particular nature of Traherne's spiritual experience. As a Christian mystic he is unusual in that despite his references to a time when his mind was so limited and blind that his

> Thoughts Extensions were:
> Like Steps and Paces they did still appear,[18]

finding God is for him not necessarily a long and difficult process, but the inevitable result of an exercise of spiritual sight, a strong and natural faculty of the human soul:

> The Highest Things are Easiest to be shewn,
> And only capable of being *Known*.
>
> . . . .
>
> Its [the sun's] very Brightness makes it neer the Ey,
> Tho many thousand Leagues beyond the Skie.
> Its Beams by violence
> Invade, and ravish distant Sence.[19]

When Traherne describes in *Nature* the soaring of his soul through space and time from one object to another, yet states that

> These all in Order present unto Me
> My Happy Eys did in a Moment see,

the reader realizes that the space flights of the poet's imagination are always liable to deepen into mystical experiences in a universe in which distance is abolished and time is unknown, a universe in which space itself is the vehicle of Deity.

In mystical writing God is symbolized by air as well as by water, for as the soul is immersed and saturated in the Divine Ocean, so it is surrounded by and filled with the Divine Wind. Thus when Traherne declares that "The Air was made to pleas / The Souls of Men" and asks, "Can Mortals breath / FELICITY!"[20] he is using a traditional symbol in a traditional way. But his representation of God as Space, though it is an extension of his use of the air and ocean symbols, emphasizes God's infinity and eternity rather than His regenerating power and His purifying love. Most mystics are content to compare His vastness with the immensity of the sea, but to Traherne's insatiable soul an ocean of water seems inadequate for such a

---

18. *Desire*, ll. 16–17.
19. *The Demonstration*, ll. 1–2, 11–14.
20. *The Estate*, ll. 60–61; *Admiration*, ll. 6–7.

comparison, and he generally discards it in favour of the unbounded ocean of space. One can follow the natural flow of his
thought from water to space in the poem *Silence*, where after
calling God "an Ocean of Delights" and himself "the Ocean of
his Pleasures", he continues:

> A vast and Infinit Capacitie,
> Did make my Bosom like the Deitie,
> In Whose Mysterious and Celestial Mind
> All Ages and all Worlds together shind.
>
> . . . .
>
> The World was more in me, then I in it.
> The King of Glory in my Soul did sit.
>
> . . . .
>
> For so my Spirit was an Endless Sphere,
> Like God himself, and Heaven and Earth was there.

As one would expect, space takes the place of the ocean
as a symbol for both God and his own soul, but this passage is
bolder than the lines preceding it, because there is an even clearer
failure to distinguish during the moment of mystical experience
between God, the infinite and eternal universe, and himself.
At such a moment his faculty of spiritual sight seems to have
divine power to contain the infinite and eternal universe within
the mind or soul, and he identifies God and his soul with the
spacious world within them both. Moreover, "la conscience
égocentrique de Traherne ne se projette pas dans cet univers
illimité pour s'y perdre ou pour y demeurer errante, mais bien
pour l'absorber";[21] he takes far greater delight in the Deity
within him than in the Deity above or without him, and paradoxically his self-consciousness is strongest when he feels closest
to the Divine. In the poem *On News* he describes his mistaken
search for Felicity

> beyond the Seas,
> Or els in som thing near at hand
> I knew not yet,

instead of in that spaciousness of his own "Glorious Soul" which
is thus further celebrated in *An Hymne upon St Bartholomews Day*:

---

21. Robert Ellrodt, *L'inspiration personnelle et l'esprit du temps chez les poètes métaphysiques anglais*, première partie, II (Paris, 1960), 338.

An Inward Omnipresence here,
Mysteriously like His with in me stands;
   Whose Knowledg is a Sacred Sphere,
That in it self at once Includes all Lands.

. . . .

Within My Self from East to West I move.

Indeed, some critics have concluded that his mysticism is not truly Christian because the centre of his interest often appears to be the self which has been exalted rather than the greater Self Which deigns to exalt.

According to Traherne's circulation theory, man's soul is most pleasing to God when it expands indefinitely and becomes

Intelligible, Endless, yet a Sphere
Substantial too: In which all Things appear,[22]

since it can then give back to Him the whole universe all at once and best fulfil its part in the great circular movement. The many possibilities for the use of the circle symbol are never far from the mind of this lover of infinity and eternity, and it is natural that he should associate the circle with infinite and eternal space. Thus he consistently refers to the souls of God and man as spherical in shape and yet at the same time filled with endless space. Such a conception of God was conventional enough in the seventeenth century, for the definition of Him as "a Circle, whose Circumference is nowhere and whose Centre everywhere",[23] had become a theological platitude. But equally persistent was the idea that the soul of man, though spherical, is but a little copy of the Great Circle, like the drop of dew in Marvell's poem; and indeed few poets of the period would have wished to break the circumferences of their souls' circles and push out into endless space because they were "charmed by the small" and "fearful of the vast, the unlimited, the unpatterned".[24] Traherne, however, feeling no such fears, and by nature incapable of accepting finite limits, describes his own spirit in terms which most Christians would use only for God:

---

22. *Thoughts* III, ll. 69–70.
23. Nicolson, *op. cit.*, p. 47.
24. *Ibid.*, pp. 57, 168–69.

A Strange Extended Orb of Joy,
Proceeding from within,
Which did on evry side convey
It self, and being nigh of Kin
To God did evry Way
Dilate it self even in an Instant, and
Like an Indivisible Centre Stand
At once Surrounding all Eternitie.
Twas not a Sphere
Yet did appear
One infinit. Twas somwhat evry where.[25]

One is conscious here of his difficulty in describing his experience. Like the earlier poets he loves the circle symbol, but his feeling of the absence of bounds of any shape impels him to use it in a different way; the paradox of an "Orb of Joy" which yet was "not a Sphere" clearly arises from his vision of a circle everywhere extended and drawing everything into the unity of its own being.

In the seventeenth century "man was beginning to apply to an expanded universe adjectives and epithets long reserved for Deity, appropriate alone to the Incomprehensible",[26] but this mystic goes even further. "La plus grande hardiesse de Traherne . . . est de prêter à l'homme des facultés infinies; mieux encore, d'en faire le centre et la circonférence de l'infinité, de cette infinité même qui serait l'essence éternelle de la Divinité."[27] Nevertheless, his bold idea of the human soul as a sphere of endless space is closely related not only to his use of the ocean symbol but also to his use of light symbols. When his mystic journey is ended and he meets "Eternal Bliss", "The obscure shady face / Of endless Space"[28] within him becomes an endless "Sphere of Light"[29] shining like the sun with Wisdom and Truth, or "Subtile and unbounded Air"[30] filled with the "Subtile Light"[31] that has broken through the veil of the finite body. Like the mind of God, this soul illumines "All Ages and all

25. *My Spirit*, ll. 86–96.
26. Nicolson, *op. cit.*, p. 175.
27. Ellrodt, *op. cit.*, première partie, II, 343.
28. *Insatiableness* I, ll. 30, 27–28.
29. *My Spirit*, l. 103.
30. *Ibid.*, l. 106.
31. *Nature*, l. 23.

Worlds",[32] which are mirrored all at once in its spacious sphere, and it may therefore be called "an Interminable Orb of *Sight*".[33] Traherne's purpose in life was to find Felicity, and he sought and found it in the Infinity and Eternity within himself. His passion for the vast is consistently expressed in the symbols he uses to describe his own soul: star, water-drop, and little circle are expanded to sun, fountain or ocean, and space itself. To him, the "Spiritual Room of the Mind" is "an infinite sphere in a point, an immensity in a centre, an eternity in a moment".[34]

---

32. *Silence*, l. 78.
33. *The Preparative*, l. 16.
34. Quoted from *Christian Ethicks* by Q. Iredale in *Thomas Traherne* (Oxford, 1935), p. 60.

V

CHILD

... Infinit is the first Thing which is naturaly Known. Bounds and Limits are Discerned only in a Secondary Maner.

(Traherne: *Centuries* II, 81)

THE CHILD IS THE SYMBOL MOST FREQUENTLY USED BY
Traherne, for nearly every poem he wrote is either based
on it or bears reference to it. One cannot therefore hope
to understand his poetry very deeply until the full implications
of his use of this traditional symbol have been grasped. Indeed,
the poet seems to have taken for his text the words of Christ in
Mark 10 : 15: "Verily I say unto you, Whosoever shall not receive
the kingdom of God as a little child, he shall not enter therein."
A believer's concept of himself as a child of God follows inevitably from his natural concept of God as his Father, the Person
Who created him and Who is thus intimately related to his soul;
and in the seventeenth century it was strengthened by the pre-
valence of the Neo-Platonic theory of the soul's original purity
and the consequent innocence of childhood. Thus Traherne is
not the only poet of his time to picture childhood as an ideal
state of being, and the thought of many of his poems could be
summed up by the opening lines of Vaughan's *The Retreate*:

> Happy those early dayes! when I
> Shin'd in my Angell-infancy.

But unlike Vaughan he feels no yearning for the past, because
he has become a "child" again and experiences in adulthood a
spiritual richness beyond the reach of the literal child, a richness
gained by conscious and persistent pursuit of that Felicity which
he was sure that he had formerly enjoyed. Traherne's mysticism,
though highly philosophical, has its seeds in the intuitions of
his own childhood; and since he nearly always presents himself
as the child figure, it is rarely easy for the reader to separate the

symbolic from the literal child. The problem is further complicated by the fact that when writing of his own childhood the poet seems to imagine as much as he remembers, sometimes attributing to the newly-born the mystical experiences of his adulthood.

There are, however, sufficient references in his poems to the superiority of his adult life to his "unexperienc'd Infancy"[1] for the reader to be assured that Traherne's use of the idealized child figure is generally consciously symbolic, in part at least. For example, in *The Approach* he even says that in childhood, God "cold Acceptance in us ever finds"; while in *Right Apprehension* he explains that

> What Newness once suggested to,
> Now clearer Reason doth improv, my View:
> By Novelty my Soul was taught
> At first; but now Reality my Thought
> Inspires.

Nevertheless, *The World* contains some interesting lines which may indicate that he believes that as a child he was spiritually more highly developed than other children:

> A Royal Crown, inlaid with precious Stones,
> Did less surprize
> The Infant Eys
> Of many other little Ones,
> Than the great Beauties of this Frame,
> . . . .
> Mine Eys did take.

This is perhaps the basis for his tendency to make such great claims for his own early intuitions; and indeed in *The Improvment* he suddenly feels the need to remind himself that at first he

> had not yet the Eye
> The Apprehension, or Intelligence
> Of Things so very Great Divine and High.

Moreover, it is surprising to find that despite his deep respect for the sanctity of childhood, Traherne is capable of using the child figure as St. Paul does in I Corinthians 3 : 1–2—to symbolize the spiritually immature Christian as opposed to the spiritual

---

1. *Shadows in the Water*, l. 1.

F

man, the mature son of God. Thus in *Blisse* he speaks derogatively of "Childish Joys" and of "foolish Men, / Grown mad with Custom" who are really "more Boys tho Men"; and in *Walking* he pictures spiritual progress as a journey from the little child's perception of the "rich and glorious things" of nature to "a Sight / Which perfect Manhood may delight".

In mystical literature, vital symbols of progress such as the seldom-used one of the immature child growing into spiritual manhood are congruent with the concept of conversion as regeneration, and regeneration may be regarded as the governing motif of Traherne's poetry. However, he more typically represents the perfect life not as a journey along a straight path from childhood to manhood but as a circular journey from childhood to childhood. He sees his own life as "a Circle of Delights",[2] for he states in *The Return*: "To Infancy, O Lord, again I com", and this is the fulfilment of his purpose as expressed at the end of *Innocence*: "I must becom a Child again." The fact that he is already spiritually childlike in adulthood before he begins to write about his life lends a mystical colouring to his descriptions of his physical infancy but at the same time precludes sentimentalism. Indeed, some readers feel that Traherne in one sense never ceased being a child, and that this accounts for the comparative lack of difficulty which he experienced in his mystical life.

To appreciate fully the essentially individual quality of Traherne's vision of the childlike state, it is helpful first to consider the traditional uses of the child symbol in the poems of more orthodox seventeenth-century Christians. Herbert never presents an idealized picture of himself as a child of God; rather is he aware of the presence of another Person Who, though so far above himself, yet is deeply concerned for his welfare and reasons with him as a loving, patient, and understanding father would with a stubborn, wayward son who must be constantly reminded of his debt to his father and of the limitations of his thinking. In *Dialogue*, the "Sweetest Saviour" stresses the weakness and inferiority of man's position thus:

> What, Child, is the ballance thine,
> Thine the poise and measure?

and man enters into a right relationship with God only when he

---

2. *The Review* II, l. 9.

self-consciousness tends to make his world a self-centred rather than a God-centred one; he is more aware of the spiritual presence of natural objects than of his Father; his God is firstly a Giver of gifts and only secondly a Person, and His fatherly love is felt mostly through His great gift, the created world. Furthermore, the child of Traherne's poems lives in such a self-contained, stable world and is governed by such pure instincts that trust in and obedience to a higher and wiser Mind are hardly necessary and fatherly discipline is unknown. Such comparative independence is the result of a natural command over unlimited spiritual and emotional resources through the direct and immediate vision of reality, and the most important truth which the child sees is the greatness of his heritage, for it is his innate sense of his spiritual possession of all things that leads him spontaneously to seek the source in God.

There are two qualities which Herbert thinks the true child of God should have, and which Traherne attributes to his child figure—contentment and humility:

> No inward Inclination did I feel
> To Avarice or Pride: My Soul did kneel
> In Admiration all the Day.[8]

Certainly, Traherne is very conscious of the potential danger in the possession of material wealth; so much so, that at the beginning of his serious search for Felicity, he "chose rather to liv upon 10 pounds a yeer . . . : then to keep many thousands per Annums",[9] and at times he seems to condemn the very principle of private material ownership, as when he speaks of "Cursd and Devisd Proprieties".[10] But although his child figure could not be accused of avarice in the ordinary sense, his idea of contentment is very different from Herbert's, for it is based not on the bounding of possessive desires but on the perfect satisfaction of boundless desires for the spiritual possession of everything:

> A quiet Mind is worse than Poverty!
> Unless it from Enjoyment spring!
> . . . .
> Life! Life is all: in its most full extent
> Stretcht out to all things, and with all Content![11]

---

8. *Innocence*, ll. 25–27.
9. *Centuries* III, 46.
10. *Wonder*, l. 49.
11. "Contentment is a sleepy thing!", ll. 3–4, 26–27.

Similarly, Traherne's child feels no pride arising from material possession, and is humble enough to give constant expression to wonder arising from his God-given faculty of spiritual possession; yet in the very expression of this wonder there is an emphasis on the exalted self which is foreign to traditional Christian ideas of humility. Thus in *The Rapture* the mystic expresses the joy of the recovery of childlikeness in exclamations such as

> How Great am I,
> Whom all the World doth magnifie!

and "O how Divine / Am I!" One may undoubtedly detect in his writings "une avidité de faveurs divines et de biens spirituels, un orgueil—disons même une naïve satisfaction—à se sentir élevé, glorifié, déifié";[12] and since he is convinced that his own "Heavenly Avarice"[13] is a great virtue given to him by God, it is naturally reflected in the symbolic child of his poems, the child who is also Traherne himself.

In *The Retreate*, Vaughan seems to associate the child's purity with his vision of nature's glory by speaking of his own "Angell-infancy"

> When on some *gilded Cloud*, or *flowre*
> My gazing soul would dwell an houre,
> And in those weaker glories spy
> Some shadows of eternity,

and one is easily reminded of the opening of *Wonder*. The resemblance is merely superficial, however. Vaughan never shows any tendency to identify innocence with purity of vision as Traherne does. The somewhat Platonic child of *The Retreate* sees "shadows of eternity" in natural objects primarily because he has just left the eternal realm and still remembers its greater glory, while the sinless child of *Wonder*, wholly occupied with the present, sees by the free exercise of his natural gift of clear spiritual sight that "The World resembled [God's] *Eternitie*", and cannot imagine greater glories than "all the Works of GOD so Bright and pure, / So Rich and Great".

Traherne's idealized child figure discerns three great

---

12. Robert Ellrodt, *L'inspiration personnelle et l'esprit du temps chez les poètes métaphysiques anglais*, première partie, II (Paris, 1960), 364.
13. *Desire*, l. 8.

mystical truths: that all things are God's gifts to him, that the spiritual is in the material, and that all things are boundless. This association of mystical insight with childhood simplicity leads the poet at times to combine two of his symbols for the pure soul into one term, "Infant-Ey", and indeed the original subtitle of *Poems of Felicity* is "*Divine Reflections*" *On The Native Objects of* "*An Infant-Ey*". The poem *An Infant-Ey*, which laments the temporary loss of his childhood vision through sin, shows clearly that for Traherne happiness lies in the possession of the infinite and the eternal. Since his "Infant-Ey" was "A simple Light from all Contagion free", it saw "things remote as well as nigh" and he "Beheld as [his] ev'n all Eternities", but when "Wantonness and Avarice got in", his

> feeble and disabled Sense
> Reacht only Near Things with its Influence.

One of Traherne's firmest beliefs is that "Nature teacheth Nothing but the Truth",[14] while "corrupt Custom is a second Night",[15] and in *The Apostacy* he maintains that the child first sins when, influenced by the opinion of the adults around him and against the wisdom of his nature, he learns to gaze on "Som Tinsel thing whose Glittering did amaze" and becomes "A Stranger to the Shining Skies" because his eyes are now "blemisht". By far the most damaging sin of all, he thinks, is "the refusal to accept this unique and absolutely priceless gift —the world as your possession and the art of enjoying it".[16] But Traherne sees such a refusal as essentially a bounding of natural spiritual resources:

> We first by Nature all things boundless see;
> > Feel all illimited; and know
> > No Terms or Periods: But go on
> > > Throughout the Endless Throne
> Of God, to view His wide Eternity;
>
> .   .   .   .
>
> > > Tho we are taught
> > To limit and to bound our Thought.[17]

---

14. *Nature*, l. 3.
15. *Right Apprehension*, l. 8.
16. R. W. Hepburn, "Thomas Traherne: The Nature and Dignity of Imagination", *Cambridge Journal*, VI (1953), 729.
17. *The City*, ll. 61–65, 69–70.

Thus sin not only causes a limitation of vision, but also tends to be identified with such a limitation, just as innocence tends to mean pure and therefore infinite vision. Traherne's ideas about sin have much in common with the Platonic theory of sin as ignorance, and could even be considered as a personal interpretation of this theory.

Traherne's passion to possess the infinite by means of spiritual vision has already been discussed in this study, but it is significant that in the poem *Sight* he speaks of his

> Infant-Ey
> Abov the Sky
> Discerning endless Space.

Here he is probably using "Infant-Ey" in a purely figurative sense, though this is not necessarily so, since when speaking of his physical childhood in *Nature* he claims,

> My Inclinations raisd me up on high,
> And guided me to all Infinitie,

and the rest of the poem shows that his view of "Infinitie" went beyond the confines of earth and sky. The form of outer illumination which Traherne attributes to the soul of the literal child can be accepted as credible to a certain point, but the reader finds incredible such pictures of the infant's inner illumination as are found in the second section of *Innocence*, *The Preparative*, *Dumnesse*, and *Silence*. It is impossible to doubt the poet's sincerity, yet only a fairly mature mystic could have such experiences, and various explanations have been offered to account for this inconsistency. Gladys I. Wade suggests an artistic deficiency by her remark that "the ethical teaching is permitted to distort the literal picture",[18] and Robert Ellrodt, while suggesting that Traherne attributes inner illumination to his early infancy because of Platonic ideas about the child's nearness in mind, heart, and spirit to its Origin, even goes so far as to state: "Je doute toutefois qu'il ait connu l'illumination *intérieure*."[19] However, it is now known that Traherne did have such an experience, for he recounts it in his recently-discovered *Select Meditations*,[20] and it seems very likely that in his poetry he presents inner illumination as a

---

18. *Thomas Traherne: A Critical Biography* (Princeton, 1944), p. 169.
19. "Le Message de Thomas Traherne, Apôtre de la Félicité", *Cahiers du Sud*, XXXI (1950), 453.
20. See quotation p. vi, this volume.

memory from early childhood because, genuinely believing that he could remember experiencing it in infancy as well as in adulthood, he chose to attribute it to infancy to complete his literal-symbolic picture of the child of God. A psychological explanation for such a belief can be found in the fact that "Toute perception, toute intuition qui vient combler une attente s'accompagne aisément de l'impression du déjà vu",[21] and this impression would be confirmed by the influence of Neo-Platonic philosophy.

It has been shown that in Traherne, the illumination of the self, the flooding of the personality with spiritual radiance, is accompanied by a conviction of inner spaciousness and of absolute freedom from all limitations of space, time, and distance. This experience is to him perhaps the highest fulfilment of his passion for the infinite; but it is the infinite in everything, and not only in space, time, and distance, for which this mystic craves. Thus the inner sphere of the soul is pictured not as empty space, but as vastness filled with the infinite in number and variety, an ocean in which "All Ages and all Worlds together shind";[22] similarly, the greatest glory of the human mind is its infinite capacity to multiply its inner objects at will:

> We sundry Things invent,
> That may our Fancy giv content;
> See Points of Space beyond the Sky,
> And in those Points see Creatures ly.[23]

Indeed, infinity and eternity themselves interest Traherne less than the perspective of innumerable joys or unlimited possessions within them, each one of which is in itself unbounded, since "every Thing is truly Infinite".[24] Just as the infant of *The Salutation* and *Wonder* reaches out to everything to take it unto himself and rejoices that God has adorned the world for him and that all things are his if he prizes them, so the adult mystic, having regained his early felicity, sings ecstatically:

> For Me the World created was by Lov;
> For Me the Skies, the Seas, the Sun, do mov;
>   The Earth for Me doth stable stand.[25]

---

21. Ellrodt, *L'inspiration personnelle et l'esprit du temps chez les poètes métaphysiques anglais*, première partie, II (Paris, 1960), 368–69.
22. *Silence*, l. 78.
23. *Consummation*, ll. 21–24.
24. "As in a Clock", l. 31.
25. *Hosanna*, ll. 61–63.

As he reviews his life, Traherne sees a vision of his childhood as an inner paradise, "a Sphere / Wherin ten thousand hev'nly Joys appear", for in it his mature thoughts and his early instincts are united to form a perfect whole.[26] Childhood has become a symbol for his entire life "Stretcht out to all things, and with all Content";[27] he knows that he is a true son of his God—a God of Platonic plenitude Who recognizes no bounds in His creative activity and Who wishes His children to impose no restrictions on their spiritual possession of His creation. "Insatiableness is Good, but not Ingratitud",[28] and to impose such restrictions would be to commit the sin of ingratitude against God Himself.

---

26. *The Review* II, ll. 1–6.
27. "Contentment is a sleepy thing!", ll. 26–27.
28. *Centuries* I, 21.

VI
KING

Let nothing satisfy me but all Eternity,
And all within it.
                    (Traherne: *Thanksgivings for God's Attributes*)

As it is natural for a son to be his father's heir, the
Father-son relationship between God and the soul is closely
associated in Traherne's mind with the idea of inheritance.
The child who feels pure joy in everything he sees realizes
instinctively that he enters "this Eden so Divine and fair, / So
Wide and Bright" as the "Son and Heir" of the One Who created
it,[1] and that only an "Eternal Heavenly King"[2] could have the
power to create such beauty. In his eyes, all the objects around
him shine with the splendour of royal wealth inherited by him
from the King of Kings.

The common titles for God, "King" and "Lord", imply
a relationship between Him and man—that of Master and
servant. Thus most religious writers use these titles chiefly to
emphasize God's omnipotence and man's obligation to honour
and serve Him by obeying His commands. Among seventeenth-
century English poets, the pious Herbert in particular is constantly aware of his position as God's servant, even stating that
his purpose as a religious poet is to "plainly say, *My God, My
King*".[3] Traherne occasionally expresses a loyal servant's reverence
for his powerful Lord, as in *Thoughts* IV, where he pictures
"Hosts of Angels" attending at God's throne and prays: "Let
my pure Soul . . . / Attend upon thy Throne." His use of the
king symbol, however, generally has a somewhat different tone
and purpose, for he feels exalted rather than humbled by his

1. *The Salutation*, ll. 35–36.
2. *Silence*, l. 66.
3. *Jordan* I, l. 15.

service to God. When in vivid images of a royal court he speaks
of human thoughts as "Tasters to the Deitie"[4] and as

> the privileged Posts that Soar
> Unto his Throne, and there appear before
> Our selvs approach,[5]

he is celebrating not God's power and majesty but man's infinite
mental capacity. Man is glorious and pleasing to his King because,
according to Traherne's circulation theory, he is needed by God
to "taste" the created world and return it to Him in gratitude,
and also because in this life he can allow his thoughts the freedom
to "soar abov the Skie" and see "The Joys and Treasures of the
DEITIE".[6]

One traditional aspect of the King and subject relationship
which Traherne emphasizes is that the subject's service is or
should be the expression of his loving thanks to the King Who
first loved and served him and Who continues to do so. In *On
Christmas-Day* the poet refers constantly to his obligation to sing
praises to his Lord and Saviour for making the manger His
throne in order to redeem mankind, and in *Bells* he rejoices that

> His Fame
> Is gon throu-out the World, who dy'd
> Upon the Cross for me.

But Traherne's poems are rarely so specifically Christian in
content. When he thinks of loving service from or to his King
it is nearly always in terms of gifts given by and returned to Him,
and he tends to put the created world and the power of human
thought in the place of the Son and the Holy Spirit as the greatest
of the Father's gifts to man. In *The Inference* II he advises the
reader to

> Consider that for All our Lord hath don,
> All that He can receiv is this bare Sum
> Of God-like Holy Thoughts,

and from the rest of the poem it is evident that the creation of
the world is foremost in his mind when he speaks of "All our
Lord hath don", for three times he points out that God values

---

4. *Thoughts* I, l. 77.
5. *Thoughts* IV, ll. 5–7.
6. *Ibid.*, ll. 2, 12.

our thoughts more than the material universe. Characteristically, the realization of the importance of man to God gives rise to exclamations of delight:

> How glorious, how divine, how great, how good
> May we becom! How like the Deity
> In managing our Thoughts aright!

In Traherne's use of the king symbol, then, one sees the same identification of love with the giving of gifts as in his use of the child symbol. Whether God is depicted as King or as Father, He is primarily a Giver of gifts to man.

Perhaps the clearest indication of his aggressively possessive nature is in the poem *Poverty*, in which he recounts some of the thoughts of his childhood after he had been estranged from God by the customs of those around him. Having temporarily lost his conviction that everything was his, he still instinctively expected to have great wealth and was naïvely amazed at his poverty:

> I wonder'd much to see
> That all my Wealth should be
> Confin'd in such a little Room.

The source of this amazement was his intuition that if there is a loving Creator He must be infinite in His giving to each creature, since

> His Lov must surely be
> Rich, infinit, and free.

Traherne implies that these intuitions were well-founded; only his spiritual blindness, he says, prevented him from seeing the King of Kings, but now he has found Him because "*His* Works *my* Wealth became". His great discovery was that happiness lies not in material possession but in the spiritual possession of the infinite.

Since only one who is rich can give riches to others, Traherne persistently enhances his king symbolism by images of wealth, picturing the world as God's "Holy Court", a palace adorned with "Plenty of Jewels, Goods, and Treasures",[7] and holy people as "the King of Glory's Diadem".[8] To many, a

---

7. *Poverty*, ll. 47–52.
8. *Christendom*, ll. 119–20. This metaphor is borrowed from Isaiah 62 : 3.

diadem or crown is merely a symbol of power, but this poet uses it mainly as a symbol of wealth, for often, as in the last two stanzas of *The World,* he contrasts false wealth such as literal crowns and thrones with true, natural wealth. Even when he calls the world God's "Spacious *Throne*"⁹ he is emphasizing His wealth more than His ruling power over it. Traherne differs from most Christian writers in that to him "King" seems a fitting title for God chiefly because of His infinite treasures, and in *The Circulation* he gives a feudal illustration of his conviction that God is Lord by virtue of His possession and distribution of wealth:

> No Tenant can rais Corn, or pay his Rent,
> > Nor can even hav a Lord,
> That has no Land.

"Land" may represent all God's gifts, but in the poems based on his circulation theory Traherne refers especially to the visible creation. By contrast, Herbert in *Redemption* uses the commercial and legal terms of feudalism to refer specifically to purely spiritual gifts, for the "new small-rented lease" is the redemption offered by the New Covenant. Furthermore, the dramatic ending highlights the willing suffering of the "rich Lord" for His tenants— His earthly poverty and the costly sacrifice of Himself so that they might be spiritually rich. Herbert's conception of God is wholly traditional. His Lord, though supremely powerful, expresses His love for man primarily through His choice of suffering.

In his poetry, however, Traherne does not dwell on the Lord's suffering, but rather on His supreme felicity; and even his attitude to the cross is somewhat different from that of most Christians, as is shown by the following passage:

> His Grievous Cross is a Supreme Delight,
> And of all Heavenly ones the greatest Sight.
> His Throne is neer, tis just before our face,
> And all Eternitie his Dwelling place.
> His Dwelling place is full of Joys and Pleasures,
> His Throne a fountain of Eternal Treasures.¹⁰

Although Christ's crucifixion is commonly regarded as a crown-

---

9. *The Improvment,* l. 42.
10. *Thoughts* IV, ll. 77–82.

ing triumph and as a great cause for thanksgiving, only a "Christian Epicurean" could so disregard the anguish of the Passion as to call the cross "a Supreme Delight" and to turn his mind easily from it to a throne valued chiefly as "a fountain of Eternal Treasures". How closely he associates Christ's cross with the wealthy power of His kingship is suggested also by his claim that "To this poor Bleeding Naked Man did all the Corn and Wine and Oyl, and Gold and Silver in the World minister in an Invisible Maner, even as he was exposed Lying and Dying upon the Cross", and by the command to his soul to "haste away / To Jesus THRONE, or CROSS".[11] This joyful identification of throne and cross may spring from Traherne's mystical experience coupled with his ideas about sin and circulation. For him, redemption from sin or blindness results in an illuminated vision and therefore, through spiritual possession, in a perfect participation in the great circulation of all things from and back to God; and since Christ's death makes man's redemption possible, it may be considered "a Supreme Delight" to God as well as to man, for by His death God receives back in full measure all the "Eternal Treasures" of His creation, including man himself. This attitude to the cross would be quite natural to one who could not conceive of a happiness that did not involve the glory of possession.

There are, however, many possible explanations for Traherne's almost exclusive concentration on the possessive joy of God and man and for his instinctive refusal to accept evil or to suffer it. Robert Ellrodt delves into the psychological aspects of his poetry and asserts that Traherne's habitual state could be described as spiritual euphoria because "le sentiment de joie et d'assurance semble disproportionné à la circonstance qui le produit".[12] This can be only a matter of opinion, but it is interesting to find the same thought-patterns in his picture of man as the son and heir of the King of Kings.

In *The Evidence* Traherne gives two reasons for his certainty that he is God's heir: the Bible declares that

> Eternity its self's the Pale
> Wherin my tru Estate enclosed is,

and

---

11. *Centuries* I, 60; *An Hymne upon St Bartholomews Day*, ll. 34–35.
12. *L'inspiration personnelle et l'esprit du temps chez les poètes métaphysiques anglais*, première partie, II (Paris, 1960), 371.

G

> His *Works* themselvs affirm the same
> By what they do,

for

> The Services they do,
> Aloud proclaim them *Mine*.

There are several Biblical references to true believers as God's heirs to salvation and eternal life, but it is clear that when this mystic speaks of his "great Inheritance" he is referring not so much to a purely spiritual inheritance as to the material universe and all God's creatures in it, and that "Eternity" is here identified with the material universe throughout all ages. In *The Dialogue* he widens his inheritance to include not only natural things but also "the Works of Men", maintaining that though others do not consider that they are working for him,

> Yet all their Labors by [God's] hevenly Care
> To Thee [each person], in Mind or Body, helpful are.

Thus Traherne's interpretation of the idea of inheritance is original in its emphasis on the present spiritual possession of infinite material wealth instead of on a salvation and eternal life which can only be fully experienced in the hereafter; to him, salvation implies above all the cleansing of one's physical and spiritual senses so that one can clearly see one's lordship over everything:

> For not the Objects, but the Sence
> Of Things, doth Bliss to Souls dispence,
> And make it Lord like Thee [each person].[13]

Characteristically, too, his concentration on the joys of inheritance excludes the suffering which the Christian must expect in this world. His tone is very different from St. Paul's in Romans 8 : 17, where he states that believers are "heirs of God, and joint-heirs with Christ; if so be that we suffer with him, that we may be also glorified together".

So often does Traherne speak of the exaltation of himself as God's son and heir that it is easy to gain the false impression that he suffers from delusions of grandeur and feels himself superior to everyone else. However, statements like "I alone

---

13. *Desire*, ll. 57–59.

with [God] inherit / All these Joys"[14] spring partly from his
didactic concern. His use of the first person makes his experiences
more vivid to the reader and focuses attention on the fascinating
mystery of "the inheritance multiplied" whereby each single
person may regard himself as God's sole heir. The poem beginning "To the same purpos" tells of the child's animistic feeling
of the moon following him from place to place, shining "at once
in many places", and Traherne draws from this illustration the
lesson that the moon and stars "serv wholy ev'ry One / As if
they served him alone", since God's gifts are symbols of His
love, which, like all spiritual things, transcends logic and arith-
metic:

> The life and splendour of Felicity
> . . . .
> Are so abundant, that we can
> Spare all, even all to any Man!
> And have it all our selves!
> Nay have the more![15]

"The inheritance multiplied" is a traditional Christian doctrine,
but a more conventional mystic would have stressed that each
person is sole heir to Christ's death, resurrection, and eternal life
rather than that each person is sole heir to all the world.

Whether he considers man as the King's servant or as the
King's son and heir, Traherne delights in emphasizing the great
honour which God bestows on man by exalting him to the
position of lord over the material creation, and since a king's
heir becomes a king, it is inevitable that his enthusiasm should
lead him to use the king symbol to refer to man as well as to
God. One of his declared purposes in writing poetry is to teach
his readers how to become "reall Kings",[16] and he says that one
of the great facts which the Bible taught him is "That We on
earth are Kings".[17] This is a reference to Revelation 5 : 10, which
proclaims that Christ has "made us unto our God kings and
priests: and we shall reign on the earth"; but Traherne interprets
this in accordance with his circulation theory, and with childlike
literalness, except that he is so absorbed in man's present reign

---

14. *On Christmas-Day*, ll. 93–94.
15. "Mankind is sick", ll. 64, 68–71.
16. *The Author to the Critical Peruser*, l. 34.
17. *The Bible*, l. 7.

on earth that his future glory does not concern him greatly. Thus in *The Circulation* he maintains that

> An Earthly Weight must be the Heir
> Of all those Joys, the Holy Angels Prize,
> He must a King, before a Priest becom,
> And Gifts receiv, or ever Sacrifice;

and as the purpose of *The Enquirie*, the preceding poem in the Dobell Folio Manuscript, is to show that angels take delight in God's creation, one may be sure that it in particular is included among "all those Joys, the Holy Angels Prize". It is above all the spiritual possession of the universe which crowns God, angels, and men.

In his poetry Traherne seems far more interested in man's kingship than in God's kingship, and the idea of inheritance forms a vital link between the child and king symbols as used in reference to man. God freely offers kingship to man, His heir, and the small child instinctively accepts his high position, knowing that everything is his. Speaking of his own early infancy, Traherne maintains, "I on the Earth did reign"[18] and "evry Thing / Delighted me that was their Heavnly King".[19] When his soul was corrupted by human customs, however, it lost its sense of greatness by inheritance of infinite treasures, and

> The Glorious Soul that was the King
> Made to possess them, did appear
>   A Small and little thing![20]

To him, then, salvation implies a return to childhood and therefore a return to a realization and thankful acceptance of God's gift of kingship:

> For did [men] know their Reall Interest,
>   No doubt they'd all be Kings.[21]

Moreover, he does not consider it difficult to discover

> That all we see is ours, and evry One
> Possessor of the Whole; that evry Man
> Is like a God Incarnat on the Throne,

for nature easily teaches the soul the highest truths.[22]

---

18. *Innocence*, l. 58.
19. *The Preparative*, ll. 29–30.
20. *On News*, ll. 54–56.
21. *Misapprehension*, ll. 12–13.
22. *Ease*, ll. 17–19, stanzas 1–2.

Although it is chiefly the possessive capacity of his soul that makes man king over the material universe, Traherne regards his body as regal, too, because of its physical riches; thus he sometimes uses the king symbol as well as the sun and ocean symbols to refer to the human body. In *The Person* he sets out to display the glory of the "Sacred Lims" which he addresses,

> That like Celestial Kings,
> Ye might with Ornaments of Joy
> Be always Crownd;

but he hastens to explain that he intends to "Glorify by taking all away" to reveal the naked splendour of the human form whose true "Ornaments" are its own parts. A more startling use of the king symbol is found in the passage beginning "While I, O Lord, exalted by thy hand", from *Thanksgivings for the Body*, for his assertion of human bodies that

> Beyond all heights above the World they reign,
> In thy great Throne ordained to remain

is even more forceful than his similar assertion that his soul "With God enthron'd may reign".[23] One who apprehends the immanent Deity as strongly as Traherne does sees material things partaking of the spiritual by His indwelling power.

Wealth is to him the main criterion of kingship, but he does not entirely neglect the concept of man's conquest and government over evil forces. In the poem beginning "Were all the World a Paradice of Ease" he states that we must attain principles "which will help to make us reign" over wrongs and "quell / The very Rage, and Power of Hell" (stanza 2), while in "A life of Sabbaths"[24] he speaks of conquering Satan, reigning now on earth, and being "Crownd with Victorie". Such traditional expressions are very rare in his poetry in comparison with his constant emphasis on spiritual riches; yet even in these one sees his concern with man's kingship here and now rather than in the next world.

Traherne has such an exalted vision of man's position even in this life as king of the infinite that he sometimes makes almost incredibly daring statements about the relationships between God and man. For instance, he maintains in *The Recovery* that God

---

23. *Hosanna*, l. 55.
24. *Centuries* III, 47.

"attains / His Ends while we enjoy. In us He reigns", and in *Thoughts* III that good human thoughts are "the Things wherwith even God is Crownd". These are, of course, references to his circulation theory, which stresses God's need for man, a creature who can enjoy the creation physically as well as spiritually and return it to the Creator, thus increasing His kingly happiness in the possession of everything, including man himself. To Traherne's mind, only he who reaches out to possess and enjoy the infinite can wholly please "the Father of all Infinites",[25] since all things are meaningless when considered apart from man, "the King / Made to possess them".[26]

---

25. *The Anticipation*, l. 7.
26. *On News*, ll. 54–55.

VII

MARRIAGE

BY LOV OUR SOULS ARE MARRIED AND SODDERD TO THE CREATURES:
AND IT IS OUR DUTY LIKE GOD TO BE UNITED TO THEM ALL.
                                        (TRAHERNE: *Centuries* II, 66)

SINCE THE CHIEF CONCERN OF EVERY MYSTIC IS THE DEVELOP-
ment of a close, responsive, and loving relationship between
the Divine One and his own soul, all mystical symbolism
tends toward and centres in one great concept—that of a Divine
love-union. The spiritual senses provide the means of apprehending God's relationship to the soul, normally in terms of
such symbols as light, water, father, or king, but also in terms
of human marriage if the experience of spiritual love is sufficiently
intimate and intense. The marriage symbol is the natural cul-
mination of all mystical symbols, for whether the mystic's
progress is conceived as journey, transmutation, or life-process,
his goal is always the fulfilment of love and the bearing of fruit
by a union between the Infinite and the finite.

The most common titles for God are "Father", "King",
"Lord", and "Saviour", but there are many other traditional
ways of representing Him as a Person Who cares for man. With
seventeenth-century geometric consciousness and an ever-
present awareness of the significance and beauty of the creation,
Traherne pictures the Creator as the "Great *Architect*" of a
"*Marvellous Designe*"[1] and as a "Great Workman"[2] Who has
lovingly built an infinite and eternal universe for man; similarly,
in *The Approach* he sees God as a skilful Artist Whose goodness,
long before his birth, prepared the thoughts of childhood for
him and "inlaid" them in him "With curious Art"

---

1. *The Improvment*, ll. 45, 43.
2. *Nature*, l. 70.

> That Childhood might it self alone be said,
>   My Tutor, Teacher, Guid to be,
> Instructed then even by the Deitie.

He says that in early infancy

>   a Pulpit in my Mind,
>   A Temple, and a Teacher I did find,
> With a large Text to comment on,[3]

for God is Teacher and Preacher to the soul willing to hear His voice; indeed, His instruction is the soul's chief defence against temptations in its spiritual warfare against the hosts of evil:

>   Thus was I pent within
> A Fort, Impregnable to any Sin:
> Till the Avenues being Open laid,
> Whole Legions Enterd, and the Forts Betrayd.[4]

But even when the wounded soul has been "inspird . . . with a Sence / Of forrein Vanities",[5] its great Captain tries to save it from death by the gift of His own life-blood, and thus becomes the chief Physician, patiently seeking to cure the soul and free it from all the harm caused by the "Serpents Sting".[6] In "Mankind is sick", a poem from *Christian Ethicks* which vividly describes the spiritual disease, madness, and blindness which oppress men, Traherne shows that all believers should be the physicians of others, sharing God's compassionate longing to save and heal His patients. Sometimes God and the soul are simply called "friends", as in *The Vision* and *Silence*; but whatever form of blood kinship or social tie a mystic chooses to illustrate the personal relationship between them, the symbol of marital union is never far from his mind.

If the mystic takes up the feminine or passive role in his relation to God, as he usually does, then the traditional concept of marriage includes and summarizes all the different ideas which are expressed by the other symbols of God's personality. The Father, Architect, or Workman building the world for man's home is like a husband providing a home for his wife; the Father,

---

3. *Dumnesse*, ll. 57–59.
4. *Ibid.*, ll. 53–56.
5. *Ibid.*, ll. 75–76.
6. *Eden*, l. 8.

King, Lord, Captain, or Physician protects and saves those dependent on Him as a husband protects his wife; the Father, Physician, or Friend feels for His children, patients, or friends the tenderness of a husband for his wife; the Father, King, or Lord is as generous a Giver as a husband who shares everything with his wife; the Father, King, Lord, Teacher, Captain, or Physician is to be humbly obeyed as a wife of mediaeval times was to submit herself to her husband and strive to follow his example. Moreover, in most of these images there is the underlying idea of God's sacrifice for man and man's obligation to make sacrifices for Him, just as there should be a mutually tender and sacrificial relationship between husband and wife. So comprehensive is the marriage symbol that it is difficult to use other mystical symbols without implicit or explicit reference to it; thus it is often combined with another symbol, as in the following lines in which Traherne speaks of God's protective Omnipresence as the soul's Husband and Captain:

> With soft Embraces it doth Clasp the Soul,
> And Watchfully all Enemies controul.[7]

As one would expect, God's omnipresence is here shown to be apprehended by spiritual touch. Diffuse "touch" is frequently felt as submersion in light, water, or air,[8] but intense and vivid "touch" is usually felt as the embraces and caresses of love. This is a further example of the climactic force of the marriage symbol.

Since regeneration may be regarded as the governing motif of Traherne's poetry, it is natural that he should more often picture his spiritual progress as life-process than as journey or transmutation, and one important vital symbol of progress is the spiritual romance between God and the soul which leads most directly and most obviously to the spiritual marriage. In *The Approach* he expresses amazement that God should have taken such pains to win his soul:

> He did Approach, he me did Woo
> I wonder that my God this thing would doe,

and he emphasizes God's infinite patience and forbearance in visiting his mind so often and striving to conquer it, only to be "Sleighted many a yeer":

---

7. *Thoughts* IV, ll. 85–86.
8. See pp. 53 and 65 of this volume.

> Thy Gracious Motions oft in vain
> Assaulted me: My Heart did Hard remain
> Long time: I sent my God away,
> Grievd much that he could not impart his Joy.

The traditional symbol of God as a Guest Who should be welcomed into the soul is given an original turn in *On News*, for there the child who has become alienated from Him but who yet seeks Him is ready to welcome any "News from a forrein Country" in the hope that it will prove to be "the Unknown Good", and is "Eager to Embrace / The Joyfull Tidings" "As if the Tidings were . . . / My very Joys themselvs". God's wooing of our souls is described more passionately in the poem *Another*, where again there is a strong contrast between His fervent desire for our love and our comparative indifference; while He burns with "Living, Endless, and Devouring fires", "We cold and Careless are". Nevertheless, though our love is "less then His", we have a portion of the Divine Fire of loving desire within us, so the seeking is mutual: "He seeks for ours as we do seek for his." When Traherne concentrates on the human pole of the spiritual romance he stresses the intensity of man's burning thirst for God, maintaining in *The Estate* that "Devouring fire / Doth feed and Quicken Mans Desire"

> And those Affections which we do return,
> Are like the Lov which in Himself doth burn.

In *Desire*, however, he clearly shows that this "burning Ardent fire" or "virgin Infant Flame" in the soul of man is an "Ambassador of Bliss" sent by God to prepare a place for Him, and thus from a wider viewpoint it is recognized as a manifestation of His desire for man's love.

By comparison with other mystical poets, Traherne's writings are strikingly free from erotic imagery. While showing his belief in the underlying conception of the mystic marriage, he generally refrains from using the sensuous language of physical love such as that which Crashaw constantly uses when speaking of heavenly love, as in his lines

> Thy blessed eyes breed such desire,
> I dy in love's delicious Fire. [9]

---

9. *A Song*, ll. 3–4.

Nevertheless *Love*, the only one of Traherne's poems which is based directly on the symbol of marital union between God and the individual soul, has been strongly criticized for its "unpleasant auras of association" by Gladys I. Wade, who at the same time expresses the opinion that "There is nothing anywhere else in Traherne to approach this in frigidity and poor taste".[10] A detailed study of *Love* is therefore essential for an understanding of his use of this symbol.

"O Nectar! O Delicious Stream!" is a fitting opening to an ecstatic religious love poem, for the joyousness of spiritual marriage and some idea of the very experience of union are conveyed by the use of "Nectar" to emphasize the sweetness of the taste of Divine Love, the heavenly Drink of the soul. Joyousness is further stressed by the musical imagery of lines 3 and 4, and the rest of the stanza is then devoted to praise of Divine Love in the form of exclamatory vocatives relating to His glorious riches, power, and beauty. High-sounding regal imagery expresses the exaltation of the mystic's experience, in which God and the soul become inseparable and the King and His bride may both be addressed as manifestations of Love. This combination of the king and marriage symbols is found also in *The Recovery*, where the world is described as a palace built by the Bridegroom for His queen.

The second stanza is concerned with the vision of God which he "coveted to behold" and which he now sees—that of an eternal Monarch Whose infinite love makes Him willing to give riches to his soul; and since water symbolizes Love, it is appropriate that he should refer to God as "The fountain Head of evry Thing" and His love as an endless spring of "Celestial Treasures". Characteristically, the regal imagery refers to the poet as well as to God, for he implies that he now possesses "all Kingdoms Realms and Crowns"; moreover, it is clearly a psychological necessity for him to contemplate his own exaltation to a position of friendship with the great King, a position whereby he might receive "Endless Glories" and "Honors". This stanza is therefore a striking illustration of the peculiarities and possible limitations of Traherne's mystical life. He does not seem to have experienced "union" with God in the way that some other Christian mystics have, for paradoxically the closer he comes to God, the more aware he is of his own importance

---

10. *Thomas Traherne: A Critical Biography* (Princeton, 1944), p. 173.

and of the divine favours bestowed on him. There is perhaps "communion" rather than "union" with the Infinite One, since the self is never dead, and "la pensée de Traherne se concentre moins sur l'Etre Infini . . ., que sur les manifestations innombrables et illimitées de l'infini".[11]

The omission of specific reference to Christ, an omission characteristic of most of Traherne's poems, is particularly unusual in a Christian love poem, and confirms the reader's opinion that for him, the created universe tends to take the Son's place as the Way to the Father, the Creator and Giver of gifts. It is significant that the "Heavenly Avarice" for which he offers thanks in *Desire* is not so much for God Himself as for "a Paradice / Unknown", and that although he maintains in the third stanza of that poem that all the beauties of this world in themselves "cannot make [his] Heavenly Joys", in the fifth stanza he states that it is "the Sence / Of Things" that gives bliss, and lists "Sence, feeling, Taste, Complacency and Sight" as "the true and real Joys". These attitudes tend to depersonalize Traherne's God, and probably account for the comparatively infrequent use of the marriage symbol in his poetry. One cannot doubt, however, that his mystical illumination is the result of profound religious experiences of close fellowship with the Divine which taught him to use his spiritual senses to see God in everything and thus to find the "Paradice / Unknown". In the fourth stanza of *Desire* he speaks of the "Love", "Amities", "Friendships", "Bridal Joys", "Sweet Affections", and "Amicable Sweet Societie" of the spiritual realm as well as the inevitable "Honors, and Imperial Treasures". Certainly, to some extent at least, he apprehends God as a Person.

In the third stanza of *Love* Traherne becomes even more ecstatic as he describes more fully the degree of intimacy which he has felt between God and his soul. He realizes now that the fulfilment of love is unbelievably wonderful, far surpassing the greatest dreams and hopes of his spiritual "Ambition"; and as in stanza 1, the quality of his bliss is symbolized by the sweet taste of the Divine "Stream". The picture of God which he presents in the third stanza is of a tremendously powerful and superabundant masculine Force Whose showers of "Joys" form a creative link between Himself and the feminine soul of the

---

11. Robert Ellrodt, *L'inspiration personnelle et l'esprit du temps chez les poètes métaphysiques anglais*, première partie, II (Paris, 1960), 336.

mystic. The use of pagan comparisons in this and the next stanza seems incongruous to the twentieth-century reader, and though at the beginning of the poem the Divine "Stream" is called "Nectar", the drink of the gods, the references to Jove, Danae, and Ganymede come as a surprise in view of the artistic theories expressed in *The Author to the Critical Peruser*.[12] Such references to classical mythology are very rare in Traherne's poems, but those which he does use, for example, the golden chain fastened to Jove's throne,[13] are commonplaces of a century which did not separate the different branches of learning to nearly the same extent as this century does. Love bringing gold to Danae was a common secular love emblem, and such emblems were sometimes turned to more serious or even sacred use. Thus Cowley addresses Light as

> Thou Golden shower of a true *Jove*!
> Who does in thee descend, and Heav'n to Earth make
> Love![14]

Even though the union between Jove and Danae was outside the bond of legal marriage, it is very unlikely that a seventeenth-century reader would find anything offensive in Traherne's use of this myth, especially since in Christian literature God is sometimes pictured as having to take the soul by force from dominance by the powers of evil, as in Donne's sonnet beginning "Batter my heart, three person'd God" and ending with the lines

> Take mee to you, imprison mee, for I
> Except you'enthrall mee, never shall be free,
> Nor ever chast, except you ravish mee.

Traherne's identification of Love's sweet "Stream" with the shower of heavenly "Joys" from the "fountain Head" and with the "Golden Rain" from Jove not only combines light and water symbolism but, especially after the regal images like "Palaces of Gold" in stanza 2, also reminds one of his tendency to identify Christ, the "Golden Stream", with the King's rich gift of "All Ages and all Worlds" to his soul.[15] Indeed, the whole of *Love* may be satisfactorily interpreted in the light of Traherne's circulation theory, and judging by its position in the

12. See p. 4 of this volume.
13. *Fullnesse*, ll. 28–31.
14. *Hymn to Light*, ll. 7–8.
15. *Silence*, ll. 64, 67–69, 78. See previously, p. 57.

Dobell Folio Manuscript, is probably meant to be so interpreted. For example, in *The Estate* he speaks of the "Outward Objects" which God has given man "to see and Taste" so that his soul may be "a Womb / Of Praises" unto Him, and in *The Recovery* he maintains that

> Gratitude, Thanksgiving, Prais,
> A Heart returnd for all these Joys

of the creation is the "Sacrifice" whereby man can repay the Creator, for

> One Voluntary Act of Love
> Far more Delightfull to his Soul doth prove

than the creation itself. It is perhaps significant that in *Love* this philosophical mystic pictures "Joys" showering down upon his head rather than into his bosom, since Danae's "Fruitfull Womb" seems to represent his intellectual soul which produces for God holy concepts and images such as those celebrated in the *Thoughts* poems which follow. Thus he declares in *Thoughts* II that

> A Delicate and Tender Thought
> . . . .
> . is the fruit of all his Works,
> Which we conceive,
> Bring forth, and Give,

and in *Thoughts* III that thoughts are "The very Offspring of the King of Kings". However, although this application of the circulation theory somewhat depersonalizes the poem *Love*, it does not lessen its ecstatic quality, because Traherne's intellectuality is here so passionate that it has become the means to a religious experience so intensely felt that the symbol of marriage is its only adequate expression. Furthermore, like most Christian mystics, he is vividly aware of the joyful sacrifice of spiritual child-bearing which the mystic marriage of God and the soul involves.

It is the first half of the last stanza of *Love* in which some readers might find "unpleasant auras of association" because of the homosexual implications of the story of Jove and Ganymede, and this raises the problem of sex in the use of the marriage symbol, especially by a male mystic. The general rule that the mystic takes up the feminine relation to God is far from absolute.

In the ancient Wisdom-philosophy, as well as in mystical thought, the Logos is represented now under the form of one sex, now under that of the other, and as Sancta Sophia or Eternal Wisdom, the Logos is feminine and can be considered as Mother and Bride; moreover, there is a reference in St. Augustine's works to Christ as the Bride.[16] In some languages the exigencies of grammar force the mystic to make Wisdom feminine, and even in English there is a strong convention that personified abstract nouns are to be treated as feminine. Thus Traherne maintains in *Right Apprehension* that Custom "must a Trophy be / When Wisdom shall compleat her Victory".

The Designe is an interesting example of Traherne's difficulty in assigning sexes to God and his soul for the purpose of using the symbols of the spiritual romance and its consummation, the mystic marriage. The first two stanzas firmly establish the genders of Eternity and Truth as neuter and feminine respectively, and Truth is pictured as the Daughter of Eternity Whose face shines upon man and attracts his love. The depiction of Eternity as the Creator of the world (stanza 1), and the use in line 12 (as later in lines 40 and 45) of light imagery in association with Its Offspring Truth, indicate that the poet is referring in particular to God the Father and God the Son, but wishes to give man the masculine role in the spiritual romance. By the third stanza he becomes confused and begins to speak of Truth as "it" instead of "she", and this confusion is found in the following two stanzas also, though at the same time Truth is called "the Great Queen / Of Bliss" Whom we are "led to Woo" so that we might "as chast Virgins Early with it joyn". However, after this clear use of marital symbolism with man as the masculine partner, he again firmly establishes the femininity of Truth, and for the first time even changes the gender of Eternity from neuter to feminine:

> Truth her [Eternity's] Daughter is my chiefest Bride,
> Her Daughter Truth's my chiefest Pride.

Any offensiveness there may be in the last stanza of *Love* is caused by the fact that while still implying a relationship of married love with God, Traherne speaks of his own soul as masculine, but fails to adjust the role of God accordingly. Nevertheless, it is easy to understand how a mystic whose awareness

---

16. Mary Anita Ewer, *A Survey of Mystical Symbolism* (London, 1933), pp. 166, 175.

of the Divine is matched by self-awareness could feel over-whelmed by the immensely superior power of the Infinite One, yet at the same time be so conscious of the unbounded powers of his own intensely active soul that he would find difficulty in thinking of himself as feminine in spirit; and in his use of the Ganymede myth there is the same delightful naïveté as is found in those poems which celebrate the "odours" of the human body.[17] Moreover, apart from the choice of sex, the comparison of God and his soul with Jove and Ganymede is very apt. Jove, the king of heaven, loved the shepherd Ganymede so much that he came down and took him up to mix the winecups and supply him with nectar in heaven. As a priestly shepherd, Traherne's task is to "fill, and taste, and give, and Drink the Cup" of the holy communion with God and His followers, the communion of the sweet wine of God's life-blood; and if seen in the light of his circulation theory, this communion cup represents primarily the sharing between God and man of the created world in which God manifests Himself, for man "tastes" God's love as revealed in His gifts and supplies Him with the nectar of pure and loving thoughts occasioned by these gifts. In the next poem, *Thoughts* I, he compares thoughts to bees sucking the sweet from flowers "As Tasters to the Deitie", and he begins another poem by addressing thoughts as "Ye hidden Nectars, which my GOD doth drink". It is possible, then, that by using the Ganymede myth Traherne means to compare the mystic marriage with a warm Platonic relationship which gives birth to good thoughts.

After commenting on the "poor taste" of the poem *Love*, Gladys I. Wade adds that the last few lines "regain a measure of dignity and sincerity"[18]—which implies that the previous lines are undignified and insincere. However, Traherne's own view stated in the "sincere" lines is that all the comparisons he has used are pitifully inadequate attempts to express something of the quality of "The true Mysterious Depths of Blessedness", for one fundamental mystical conviction is that "the intimate nearness between God and the soul is so close and so intense that no possible earthly intimacy used as an analogy can be anything but an extreme understatement of it".[19] Answers to Wade's charge of "poor taste" can be found in Traherne's claim that

---

17. See pp. 16–18, this volume.
18. *Loc. cit.*
19. Ewer, *op. cit.*, p. 144.

> Desire and Love
> Must in the height of all their Rapture move,
> Where there is true Felicity,[20]

and in Herbert J. C. Grierson's comments on *Love*: "Such audacious ecstasies transcend the limits of average humanity, which is more at home with the fearful joys of Herbert and Vaughan, or the more sensuous and remote ecstasies of Crashaw, but they are not in Traherne less profoundly religious."[21] The passionate pleasure he feels in being God's "Life" and "Joy", which leads him to end the poem with the crescendo effect of a recitation of the exalted positions God has given him in relation to Himself, is a "profoundly religious" pleasure because it is dedicated to noble ends and because it springs partly from the fulfilment of his need for God, and partly from his loving desire to respond to God's need for his soul and from his conviction that he is satisfying His need.

One of the greatest advantages of the romance symbol is that it points toward a non-static goal—the bearing of fruit through a marriage of the soul with God. This same idea, however, can be expressed in non-human terms by using the "garden" type of vital progress symbolism whereby the growth of the individual soul is represented as that of a garden, a vine, or a branch. In a contrast between the earth's fertile soil and man's hardened and barren heart which refuses to admit God, Traherne says that

> no Fruit grows
> In his Obduratness nor yields
> Obedience to the Hevens like the Fields,[22]

though in *Dumnesse* he refers to the good soil of human nature which nourishes the first impressions of infancy. The fruit which the garden of the soul can yield in response to God's love is "the fine and Curious Flower"[23] of good thought, which in turn yields more fruit in the form of good actions, for "Holy Affections, grateful Sentiments, / Good Resolutions, virtuous Intents" are "Seed-plots of activ Piety".[24] His picture in *Goodnesse* of the

---

20. "Contentment is a sleepy thing!", ll. 19–21.
21. *The First Half of the Seventeenth Century* (Edinburgh and London, 1906), p. 174.
22. *Right Apprehension*, ll. 70–72.
23. *Thoughts* II, l. 7.
24. *The Inference* II, ll. 15–17.

H

people of God as vines glorified by the Sun's beams and bearing grapes which ripen in response to His warmth implies the fruitful unity of the individual soul or vine not only with God but also with other believers, since in a vineyard the branches of the vines intertwine. Indeed the vine, though sometimes used to symbolize one soul, by tradition more often represents the corporate unity in God of all faithful ones; and in the poem *On Christmas-Day* Traherne uses both meanings. In the third stanza he instructs his soul to

> Let pleasant Branches still be seen
> Adorning thee, both quick and green;
> And . . . .
> Be laden all the Year with Fruits;
> > Inserted into Him,
> > > For ever spring,

while in the seventh stanza he prays,

> Among the rest let me be seen
> A living Branch and always green;

the life and health of the vine and its branches is dependent on the intimacy of its contact with Christ. Similarly, the individual believer may think of himself as a member spiritually joined with all the other members to form one body married to God, "the Bride / Of God *His Church*",[25] and in "Mankind is sick" the poet urges all Christians to treat others as "Our Brides, our Friends, our fellow-members".

Throughout his poetry there is abundant evidence that as a mystic Traherne is preoccupied with the idea of spiritual oneness. God, he says, is Simple, Infinite, and Eternal Being,[26] and man can unify his being so that his soul becomes "One / With in it self",[27] "Simple like the Deitie".[28] The most wonderful mystery to him is the unity of all the millions of infinite ones within the Being of the One Infinite so that "all by each, and each by all possest, / Are intermutual Joys".[29] The impulse behind all his thinking and writing is the passion for the infinite that exalts mankind to a status of kinship with God, but his apprehension

---

25. *Felicity*, ll. 13–14.
26. *My Spirit*, stanza 6.
27. *Dumnesse*, ll. 29–30.
28. *My Spirit*, l. 15.
29. *Ease*, ll. 27–28.

of Reality as more immanent than transcendent leads him to achieve a type of Divine love-union more with the Infinite One as revealed in the infinity of the material universe than with the Person of the Infinite One as revealed in Jesus Christ. Thus even when he uses the language of human love in passionate mystical poems like *Love*, his God seems to lack something of the immediate personal reality of Herbert's God. Indeed, the last stanzas of *The Designe* clearly show that for him possession of Truth tends to mean spiritual possession of the world, for the thought of Truth as his "chiefest Bride" leads to the exclamation, "How soon am I of all possest!" In conventional Christianity God the Son is the great High Priest or Mediator guiding man to Heaven; in Traherne's poems, the treasures of the universe are often treated as almost sufficient in themselves to act as mediator:

> The Heavens were an Orakle, and spake
> *Divinity*: The Earth did undertake
> The office of a Priest; And . . .
> . . . . All things did com
> With Voices and Instructions.[30]

The inevitable outcome is that some of his experiences are described as a marriage of his soul with God's creation. In *Thoughts* III he says that thought is "Queen of all things" and "shall be Married ever unto all: / And all Embrace", while in *Hosanna* he rejoices that

> All things in their proper place
> My Soul doth best embrace,
> Extends its Arms beyond the Seas,
> Abov the Hevens its self can pleas.

In this kind of communion with the immanent and infinite God, however, man or even self remains the centre of the universe,[31] and it is interesting to find that at least in one place Traherne himself seems to express a slight doubt as to whether even the intense mystical experience described in *My Spirit* is really the highest possible one. In the midst of an ecstatic review of the vision that was granted to him of his own soul in its relationship to God and His universe, he claims that his soul appeared to be

---

30. *Dumnesse*, ll. 63–67.
31. *Hosanna*, l. 24.

My Power exerted, or my Perfect Being,
If not Enjoying, yet an Act of Seeing.[32]

Elsewhere in his work, "Enjoying" is equated with "Seeing".

---

32. *Fullnesse*, ll. 9–10.

VIII

TRAHERNE

SYMBOLIST and POET

IT IS REMARKABLE THAT A MAN WHO HAS CONCEIVED SUCH BEAUTIFUL
IDEAS SHOULD ALLOW HIMSELF TO BE SO AWKWARD IN THEIR EXECUTION.
(MENDELSSOHN ON SCHUMANN)

IN ALL THE FOREGOING CHAPTERS THE EMPHASIS HAS BEEN ON
the meaning Traherne gives to the traditional symbols in his
poetry and on their wider significance in relation to his
mysticism, philosophy, and personality. There is, however,
another important aspect of his mystical symbolism: its relation
to the literary quality of his poems, and in particular to imagery
and structure. No one can deny that as a poet Traherne has many
technical faults, such as his frequent use of the expletive "do";
yet I believe that most of his poems have sufficient artistic merit
to justify an attempt to understand them as works of art. This
chapter, then, is a descriptive rather than an evaluative study of
the aesthetic result of his symbolic vision.

One of the most striking differences between other seventeenth-century religious poets and Traherne is the virtual lack
of specifically Christian symbolism in his poems, so that the
casual reader who turns from Herbert to Traherne may well
find it difficult at first to recognize the latter's broader and more
general symbols. However, Traherne's vision of life, though
different, is not less deeply symbolic, for he sought after the
Divine as revealed not in Church creeds and symbols but in
nature and in the mind of man. He saw the whole world as the
outward form of an inner Reality Which is essentially God, for
to such an illuminated mind the material is sacramentally the
vehicle of the spiritual. Thus the reader who is sensitive to the
rhythm of Traherne's spirit is constantly aware of the "something
more" or the "something beyond" gleaming through such
apparently simple descriptions of nature as the following one of
the sun in *The World*:

> He shed his Beams
> In golden Streams
> That did illustrat all the Sky;
> Those Floods of Light which he displays,
> Did fill the glittr'ing Ways,
> While that unsufferable piercing Ey
> The Ground did glorify.

Perfect union of the literal and the symbolic through imagery is not uncommon in Traherne's poems, and even his most literal lines are tinged with an otherworldliness that tends to give ordinary images the force of symbols. This tendency is reinforced by two factors: the sources from which the images are drawn, and the way in which they are used.

Traherne's choice of universal nature symbols like light, water, and space, which are very vague in comparison with more precise symbols such as Herbert's bunch of grapes, is consistent with his choice of the great "creatures" like sun, sea, air and sky and fields as his major stock of nature images, for his soul delighted in vastness and spaciousness filled with the glory of light. Closely associated with these greater "creatures" are stars, fountains and streams, and trees, while towering above them all is the miracle of the human body, whose senses, perfectly equipped to enjoy all the creation which serves man, often become symbols of spiritual senses. In itself, the large scale of most of Traherne's images in contrast with "smaller" images such as that of the flat map in Donne's *Hymne to God my God, in my sicknesse* gives them a generality which moves them somewhat towards the realm of symbolic meaning, and their simple and obvious derivation from major symbols tends to give them something of the tone and flavour of those symbols, even in quite literal passages such as this:

> How easy is it to believ the Skie
> Is Wide and Great and fair? How soon may we
> Be made to know the Sun is Bright and High,
> And very Glorious, when its Beams we see?[1]

Traherne's favourite small-scale images are of shining metals and jewels, especially gold, silver, pearls, rubies, diamonds, and emeralds, and there can be no doubt that he felt a very keen

---

1. *Ease*, ll. 9–12.

sense-delight in colour, glittering movement, and brilliance. However, it is clear that his use of these images is primarily symbolic, for he closely relates them to light symbolism, as in *The Odour*,[2] and to regal symbolism, as in *Adam*:

> He crowned was with Heven abov,
> Supported with the Foot-stool of God's Throne,
> A Globe more rich than Gold or precious Stone.

Moreover, metals and jewels are not mentioned for their own sake so much as to evoke an impression of the richness and splendour of the world, "A Mine, a Garden, of Delights" with which they are often unfavourably contrasted:

> For so when first I in the Summer-fields
>   Saw golden Corn
>   The Earth adorn,
>
> . . . .
>
>   No Rubies could more take mine Ey;
>   Nor Pearls of price,
>   By man's Device
>   In Gold set artificially,
>   Could of more worth appear to me.[3]

"As objects, indeed, gold and silver and rubies were nothing to him, but as words, they had a very different value, through their frequent use in the poetical books of the Old Testament to symbolise all that is precious."[4]

Even when speaking of small things, Traherne has the special gift of endowing his lines with a sense of unworldly spaciousness. In the context of the following lines from *The Salutation*, his use of the adjective "azure" evokes the sky and its infinity:

> Their Organized Joynts, and Azure Veins
> More Wealth include, then all the World contains.

---

2.   These Hands are Jewels to the Ey,
. . . .
Can Jewels solid be, tho they do shine?
. . . .
Ye solid are, and yet do Light dispence.
See p. 23, this volume.
3. *The World*, ll. 89, 37–39, 41–45.
4. Gladys E. Willett, *Traherne (An Essay)* (Cambridge, 1919), p. 55.

Similarly, he focuses the microscope of his mystical vision and his imaginative intellect onto a grain of sand, seeing in it the infinity of God's power, wisdom, and love to mankind, a circle everywhere extended:

> In all Things, all Things service do to all:
> And thus a Sand is Endless, though most small.[5]

In his poems the cabinet-figure so common in seventeenth-century literature is made to serve a very uncommon purpose. Whereas Herbert welcomes the neat restriction of "A box where sweets compacted lie",[6] Traherne revels in the boundlessness of the universe, his vast dwelling-place filled with diverse and beautiful riches to be valued like treasures kept safely in a cabinet. Like Blake, he hated hedges, ditches, and walls;[7] not as objects in themselves, of course, but for what they symbolized to him— all the restrictions which man has wrongly imposed upon him-self. "The Spaces fild" into which his soul broke "like fire" were "like a Cabinet / Of Joys before [him] most Distinctly set";[8] but though

> The Hevens were the richly studded Case
> Which did [his] richer Wealth inclose;
>
> . . . .
> No Confines did include
> What [he] possest.[9]

While grasping one thing, his mind never forgets that there are more and more to be embraced; the "walls" of his cabinet open out to and surround infinity. Such a use of images as spring-boards to the rarefied atmosphere of spiritual space tends to elevate their function to that of symbols.

The symbolic sources of most of Traherne's images and the vastness which they possess or assume must be considered in conjunction with other aspects of his poetry, as a study of his literary style reveals that it is the combination of many facets that makes his poems such a clear reflection of his personality and of his symbolic vision. In *The Author to the Critical Peruser*, Traherne states that his aim is to share his vision of life and thus

---

5. "As in a Clock", ll. 29–30.
6. *Vertue*, l. 10.
7. See *Wonder*, stanza 7; *Christendom*, stanza 5; and *The City*, stanza 6.
8. *Nature*, ll. 73–76.
9. *The City*, ll. 41–42, 47–48.

to help his reader to find true happiness. Moreover, he is convinced that in order to make his reader see the beauty of Truth as clearly as he does, he must present it "naked" in a simple style and through "transparent Words". To a remarkable degree he abides by his aesthetic principle; hence the very bald statements in philosophical poems such as *The Anticipation*, the comparative lack of figures of speech in his poetry as a whole, and his preference for the clarity of similes as opposed to the "obscurity" of metaphors,

> For Metaphores conceal,
> And only Vapours prove.[10]

It is interesting to note, however, that in the very act of condemning metaphors he unconsciously uses one by identifying them with "Vapours", for the natural thought processes of a man finely equipped with poetic perception are to some extent metaphorical. Nevertheless, there is a conspicuous absence from his lines of the conceits which are so characteristic of the seventeenth-century metaphysical poets, since he is resolved that nothing shall distract the reader's attention from what he is saying, which is to him all-important. Words in themselves hold little fascination for him; undoubtedly he is, as T. S. Eliot has pointed out, "more mystic than poet".[11] With an almost startling directness and an apparent spontaneity he seems to place before the reader's eyes the thoughts themselves in concrete form rather than the words expressing them. Even the favourite images so vitally related to the thoughts appear primarily as transparent filters through which Traherne's mind communicates with the reader's, for they usually lack that feeling of solidity which most people associate with the material world. The opening of *My Spirit* is a good example:

> My Naked Simple Life was I.
> That Act so Strongly Shind
> Upon the Earth, the Sea, the Skie,
> That was the Substance of My Mind.

Here the simple directness of spiritual thought robs Traherne's imagery of concreteness; the earth and the sea seem intangible.

---

10. *The Person*, ll. 25–26.
11. "Mystic and Politician as Poet: Vaughan, Traherne, Marvell, Milton", *Listener*, III (1930), 590.

Herbert, on the contrary, habitually solidifies the abstract by means of concrete imagery, as in the command to his soul, "tie up thy fears".[12]

The lack of concreteness which stems from Traherne's almost exclusive concern with ideas as opposed to their expression is but one facet of his symbolic vision. To this mystic, words are merely symbols of higher realities and must therefore be "transparent" if they are to allow the visionary light to shine through clearly; similarly, despite the keenness of his physical senses as evidenced by the intense appreciation of natural beauty which is found in nearly every poem he wrote, to him the primary interest and significance of nature lies in its revelation of higher Truth. Natural objects are valued chiefly as symbols of God's love and of His exaltation of man:

> As Tokens of his Lov they all flow down,
> Their Beauty Use and Worth the Soul do Crown;[13]

thus his poetry lacks detailed nature-observation and he is content to point to what he sees and knows, naïvely hoping that his reader will experience the same spiritual excitement as he does when the very names of favourite objects are mentioned:

> From GOD abov
> Being sent, the Heavens me enflame,
> To prais his Name.
> The Stars do move![14]

Perhaps the light in which he sees the world as a unity is so brilliant that it partially blinds him to the distinguishing features of different objects so that he fails to recognize the "thisness" of particular skies or stars as Gerard Manley Hopkins would have done. Traherne is eminently the poet of mystical illumination, and the illuminated man "often experiences the objects of nature with a new and special sensitiveness and in a singularly intimate relation to the energy of his own mind. It is in such a vision more their form and the energy of life in them that he sees than what we should ordinarily call their sensuous detail."[15] Though the importance of the material world for him lies in its communion

---

12. *The Collar*, l. 29.
13. *Thoughts* IV, ll. 69–70.
14. *The Rapture*, ll. 11–14.
15. Ruth Wallerstein, *Studies in Seventeenth-Century Poetic* (Wisconsin, 1950), p. 254.

and union with the Holy Spirit and his ardent love of nature is more spiritual and intellectual than sensuous, his nature imagery, abstract and symbolic as it is, is yet often charged with vitality and dazzling with light:

> The very Day my Spirit did inspire,
> The Worlds fair Beauty set my Soul on fire.[16]

If Traherne did see the "sensuous detail" of natural objects, he was evidently not interested in describing it; his imagination was stirred far more by the general than by the particular, and his world was a vast one of magnificent cosmic drama. It is significant that in an age when so many poets set out to define an object, an idea, an emotion, or a state of being, he seems to avoid definition, probably sensing that the definition of anything would necessarily involve its limitation, which he as a mystic refuses to accept. His imagination seizes the indefinite rather than the definite, and demands a wider range than that of the immediate scene:

> The Thoughts of Men appear
> Freely to mov within a Sphere
> Of endless Reach; and run,
> Tho in the Soul, beyond the Sun.
> The Ground on which they acted be
> Is unobserv'd Infinity.[17]

With this setting of "unobserv'd Infinity", it is not surprising that even descriptions such as "Clouds here and there like Winged Charets flying"[18] are rare in his poems, and that he prefers to speak of

> The Skies in their Magnificence,
> The Lively, Lovely Air.[19]

Lack of concreteness and particularity of imagery, however, does not necessarily mean lack of true precision. The reader of Traherne's poems is often impressed by the absolute rightness of his precise vagueness in lines like those from *The Salutation* in which the new-born child marvels at the glories of this world:

---

16. *Nature*, ll. 5–6.
17. *Consummation*, ll. 1–6.
18. *Nature*, l. 55.
19. *Wonder*, ll. 9–10.

> Such Sounds to hear, such Hands to feel, such Feet,
> Beneath the Skies, on such a Ground to meet.

In one sweep of cosmic vision his soul apprehends the mystery behind the whole universe surrounding him, the mystery which is represented by skies and ground and which can be adequately expressed only by this sacramental mention of them in an attitude of childlike wonder; he feels the Spirit which inspires nature as a whole and is "unsurpassed in his power of recreating the general spirit of beauty".[20] Furthermore, far from appearing crude, the very simplicity of his similes and metaphors usually enhances the delicate beauty of his imaginative thought, which is on such a large scale that any complexity would seem like fussy elaborateness. There is a poetic sureness of touch in his unadorned comparisons of "Seas of Life" with "Wine",[21] a fallen soul with "a dying Flame",[22] and "A Delicate and Tender Thought" with a "fine and Curious Flower".[23]

If Traherne is regarded solely from a literary point of view, T. S. Eliot's criticism that "He has not the richness and variety of imagery which poetry needs"[24] is very just. His suspicion of the artificial and his simple and coherent purpose lead him to rely too greatly on bare, non-dramatic statement which would be boring to a reader not interested in his thoughts, and to use easily intelligible symbols and readily apprehended images which in themselves cannot afford the deep pleasure of such splendidly rich images as those in Vaughan's lines comparing night with

> Gods silent, searching flight:
> When my Lords head is fill'd with dew, and all
> His locks are wet with the clear drops of night.[25]

Moreover, his repetition of favourite images in poem after poem would be merely monotonous and irritating to an unsympathetic reader of his poetry as a whole. The reasons for such repetition are easy to understand. Traherne's imagination is a curiously unbalanced one, in that in some respects it ranges much farther afield than that of most poets—"beyond the Sun", in fact—while in other respects it is seriously restricted. Many of the

---

20. Q. Iredale, *Thomas Traherne* (Oxford, 1935), p. 77.
21. *Wonder*, l. 22.
22. *The Apostacy*, l. 62.
23. *Thoughts* II, ll. 1, 7.
24. *Loc. cit.*
25. *The Night*, ll. 31–33.

common concerns of men do not interest him, for he lacks Donne's brilliant power to borrow images from the most diverse elements of life and to mould them into one. As mystic and prophet his life is almost wholly taken up with a few very great ideas which he feels compelled to share with others, and the repetitive tendencies of his enthusiastic nature are probably strengthened by an uncomfortable awareness that his verse is powerless to express the full intensity and glory of his vision. Certain images inevitably present themselves to his mind in association with beloved ideas; hence his tireless insistence on the beauty and use of common blessings such as air and light:

> The common Air and Light
> That shines, doth me a Pleasure
> And surely is my Treasure.[26]

Nevertheless, "Even the almost obsessed repetition of a relatively narrow range of themes cannot blur the cumulative effect of conviction and of glow of feeling",[27] and just as the "vagueness" of Traherne's images is often the truest expression of his symbolic vision, so their repetition, though annoying to some readers, heightens that sense of the mystery behind external phenomena which the receptive mind feels more and more keenly as the names of earth and sea and sky are recited with serious and dedicated joy. The words have taken their life from a spiritual appreciation of those natural objects whose constant presence in the poems convinces one of the fullness and richness of the symbolic meaning they have for the poet. Though a finer artist would probably have been able to communicate this meaning more clearly than does Traherne, there is a portion of it which is private and can be shared no more than the whole secret behind his engrossment with the connotations of words like "infinite" and of rhymes like "pleasure–treasure", "bower–tower", "eye–sky", and "joy–toy".[28] What can be and is communicated, however, is the mystic's feeling of entranced wonder and impassioned love.

Any poet who senses strongly that words are inadequate to express his vision would tend to resort not only to repetition

---

26. *Misapprehension*, ll. 59–61.
27. Helen C. White, *The Metaphysical Poets: A Study in Religious Experience* (New York, 1936), p. 364.
28. The present writer cannot accept the earthbound theory that Traherne's repetition of these rhymes is due to a lack of inventive skill.

of ideas and images but also to lists of words, symbols, or comparisons serving as pointers to the ineffable. Herbert constructs the whole of his sonnet *Prayer* from a series of metaphors, but shows his awareness of their inadequacy in the meaningful understatement by which he concludes that prayer is "something understood"; similarly, Shelley builds up stanza after stanza of *To a Skylark* by piling up comparisons in an attempt to illustrate the peculiar quality of the bird's song which so delights him. When the writer is "more mystic than poet", this tendency is greatly accentuated, and there are some extreme examples of it in Traherne's poetry. Sometimes his cataloguing of words, images, or symbols in parallel phrases is a powerful reflection of the pouring forth of his feeling and of the impetuous urgency of his thought as it rushes from one illustration to the next with sustained, excited exhilaration, clutching at one after another in the hope that the total effect may be somewhat nearer to a true expression of his experience than any one illustration could be. Thus in *Desire* he describes his longing for perfect felicity as

> An Eager Thirst, a burning Ardent fire,
> A virgin Infant Flame,
> A Love with which into the World I came,
> An Inward Hidden Heavenly Love,

while the whole of *Fullnesse* consists of a series of pointers to the spiritual experience described in *My Spirit*. "That Light, that Sight, that Thought", he says, is, among other things,

> The Mirror of an Endless Life,
> The Shadow of a Virgin Wife,
> A Spiritual World Standing within,
> An Univers enclosd in Skin.

However, such lists of associated or synonymous images can become irritating if the images are used as exclamatory vocatives, and some of his most intensely felt poems are seriously marred by his habit of stark apostrophe. Indeed, the first stanza of *Love*, read unsympathetically, can seem quite ludicrous:

> O God! O Bride of God! O King!
> O Soul and Crown of evry Thing!

Nevertheless, such staccato passages at the height of ecstasy are the inevitable expression of Traherne's "direct and apocalyptic inspiration" which "sought the most abrupt . . . methods possible to express its delight".[29]

Not all of the numerous lists found in Traherne's poems originate primarily in an attempt to point to the ineffable. Many are catalogues of different external objects rather than of symbols or images virtually synonymous in meaning. His insatiable spirit forces his imagination simultaneously to seize possession of numerous objects which are closely related in his inner consciousness and to hold them included within himself, revelling in the miraculous sensation of his soul's infinity. Such simultaneity of a multitude of impressions can be indicated in no other way than by rhapsodic enumeration:

> The Earth, the Seas, the Light, the Day, the Skies,
> The Sun and Stars are mine; if those I prize.[30]

Pictorial composition, with its implication of a limiting frame, is foreign to his expansive nature, which is more interested in objects as part of an infinite whole than in objects as such. At times, indeed, all things seem equally wonderful in their infinite and eternal aspects, and he heaps them up gleefully without any attempt to exercise a principle of selection:

> The World my House, the Creatures were my Goods,
> Fields, Mountains, Valleys, Woods,
> Floods, Cities, Churches, Men, for me did shine.[31]

The verbose clumsiness which results from such enthusiasm may be regarded as part of a wider tendency to a lack of restraint and is paralleled by catalogues of superlatives or of abstract qualities; thus in *The Designe* he asserts that Eternity "did prize / Things truly Greatest Brightest fairest, Best", and in *Eden* he lists as objects of delight

> Joy, Pleasure, Beauty, Kindness, Glory, Lov,
> Sleep, Day, Life, Light,
> Peace, Melody.

Like Henry More, Traherne is intoxicated with the vastness,

---

29. H. Massingham, "A Note on Thomas Traherne", *New Statesman*, IV (1914), 272.
30. *The Salutation*, ll. 29–30.
31. *Speed*, ll. 16–18.

fullness, and variety of the universe and expresses his emotions in "a language of excess".[32]

The thick clusters of subjectively associated images which are characteristic of Traherne's poems are undoubtedly an artistic fault by conventional standards, yet they contribute to the reader's overwhelming conviction of the symbolical nature of external objects in much the same way as the recurrence of favourite imagery does. Paradoxically, the atmosphere is rarefied rather than thickened by such long lists, because a distinctive impression of any one object or of the total scene is rarely offered, and the accumulation of generalities is the simplest way to achieve an effect of spacious grandeur. The spirituality of his verse is further enhanced by its uncomplicated rhythm, for the fall of the accent most frequently where one expects it makes the items named in the lists seem like symbols in a religious ritual of thanksgiving—as indeed they probably are for a mystic to whom the Light of Eternity irradiates the light of day. The unworldly, dazzling quality of much of his imagery is matched not only by the simplicity of his vocabulary, style, and rhythm but also by his instinctive avoidance of consonantal cluttering, so that the great number of liquid or voiced consonants as compared with the number of voiceless consonants "donne à l'oreille . . . l'impression d'une soie claire, d'une étoffe légère et brillante":[33]

> Rich Diamond and Pearl and Gold
> In evry Place was seen;
> Rare Splendors, Yellow, Blew, Red, White and Green,
> Mine Eys did evrywhere behold,
> Great Wonders clothd with Glory did appear,
> Amazement was my Bliss.[34]

"La transparence de l'atmosphère, le caractère idéal et abstrait des paysages, l'éclat uniforme, les touches claires et brillantes, les couleurs simples d'enluminure rappellent certains tableaux de primitifs. L'effet n'est pas recherché et savant . . . : il procède de la même naïveté, de la même pureté du regard."[35]

---

32. Marjorie Hope Nicolson, *The Breaking of the Circle: Studies in the Effect of the "New Science" upon Seventeenth-Century Poetry* (rev. ed.; New York, 1960), p. 202.
33. Robert Ellrodt, *L'inspiration personnelle et l'esprit du temps chez les poètes métaphysiques anglais*, première partie, II (Paris, 1960), 390.
34. *Wonder*, ll. 41–46.
35. Ellrodt, *loc. cit.*

Traherne's poetry is a striking illustration of how completely the worlds of spirit and sense can be fused. Not only does he transform material things into spiritual symbols before the reader's eyes, but he also "Brings down the highest Mysteries to sense"[36] through his power to illuminate spiritual abstractions by imagery which is "sensuous" in that it depends for its effect on the reader's awareness of the delights of the senses, but which nevertheless evokes little or no actual sensory response in the reader. *The Odour*, for example, is full of images whose potential sensuousness would be exploited to the full by most poets; but Traherne spiritualizes them, mainly by constantly linking objects with Biblical colouring such as jewels, wine, oil, honey, and spices in the service of an idea which displays an innocent indifference to common associations, by tethering them closely to the intellectual argument, and by enumerating them instead of solidifying them through detailed description. Few poets are capable of illuminating the sensuous by the spiritual and the spiritual by the spiritualized sensuous so that the distinctions between spirit and matter are blurred and images seem to glow with something of the power of symbols. This is one of Traherne's natural gifts born of a vision of "Both Worlds one Heven made by Lov".[37]

A union of the literal and the symbolic may result from an awareness of the spiritual significance of actual experiences as well as from an illuminated apprehension of the material world. In the seventeenth century, interest in allegory turned from what was public, external, and impersonal to a field more private, individual, and literary;[38] thus Traherne sees his own life as an allegory of the adventures of the spirit and in his use of the child symbol does not seek for boundaries between the facts of infancy and its meaning. Projecting all experience into an eternal present, he relives daily incidents in the light of a child's imaginative preoccupations so that poems like *Shadows in the Water* and *On Leaping over the Moon* become parables illustrating profounder truths. The dangers of such intimacy with the reader are not always avoided by Traherne. His intense conviction of the value of some apparently trifling experiences occasionally leads him to include details that have no significance for anyone but the poet

---

36. *The Author to the Critical Peruser*, l. 5.
37. *Hosanna*, l. 30.
38. Rosemary Freeman, *English Emblem Books* (London, 1948), p. 7.

J

himself, and as a prelude to a childhood incident one finds the
lines:

> To the same purpos; he, not long before
> Brought home from Nurse, went to the door
> To do som little thing
> He must not do within.[39]

Moreover, in the course of recounting personal experiences
he sometimes enumerates homely things which are meaningful
to him through their subjective relationship with these experiences, but which seem an almost ludicrous conglomeration to
the general reader not acquainted with the poet's early sur-
roundings. Thus in *Solitude* he speaks of being

> Remov'd from Town,
> From People, Churches, Feasts, and Holidays,
> The Sword of State, the Mayor's Gown,
> And all the Neighb'ring Boys.

Such passages are all the more striking since his references to
daily life are usually very generalized and intellectual, even at
his most personal; many even have a Biblical flavour which
takes away the homeliness they would otherwise have:

> On things that gather Rust,
> Or modish Cloaths, they fix their minds.[40]

However, Traherne's reminiscences, the meditations inspired
by them, and the details and objects associated with them are all
products of the same symbolic vision, which transmutes the
temporal to the eternal as the material to the spiritual and presents
them with a sweet gravity which springs from a naïve expectation
that the minds of others will necessarily respond to the intimate
revelations of his own.

Although Traherne sees his life as an allegory, there is
little of the emblematic in his poems because his vision fully
integrates the literal and the symbolic. Unlike the emblem writers,
he does not choose objects and incidents and impose some significance upon them; instead, he usually identifies symbol with
reality so closely that it is difficult or even impossible for the

---

39. "To the same purpos", ll. 1–4.
40. *Dissatisfaction*, ll. 53–54.

reader to separate them. The final stanza of *Innocence* powerfully identifies the poet as a child with the symbolic child:

> An Antepast of Heaven sure!
>   I on the Earth did reign.
> Within, without me, all was pure.
> I must becom a Child again.

Similarly, his statement in *Churches* I that

> The Arches built (like Hev'n) wide and high
> Shew his Magnificence and Majesty
> Whose House it is

has nothing of the moralist's deliberate equation of object with meaning that is found in Herbert's poem *The Churche-Floore*. The presence in this world of the indwelling God is felt by him so strongly and so constantly that objects and incidents appear as natural symbols without his having to manufacture them. He does not avail himself of the common seventeenth-century practice of using the titles of poems as concrete emblems to please the reader's wit and visual imagination and to provide the poet with the self-imposed discipline of a firm, neat shape beyond which his ideas must not stray. Traherne's titles, on the contrary, are nearly always abstract, and only one, *The Estate*, could be said even to approach the solid, figurative quality of Herbert's *The Pulley* or *The Collar*. The emblematic method is foreign to him.

One of the chief criticisms of Traherne's poetry is that it is undisciplined and that the individual poems therefore lack organic unity of form and content. As a symbolist he makes remarkably little use of the structural possibilities of the symbol as a unifying unit in the architecture of a poem. *The Vision* and *The Odour* have symbolic titles and are built around the symbols of vision and odour, but these symbols are so general and abstract that the recurrence of words like "see" and "sweet" seems unavoidable in the very expression of the poet's thought, and has little power as a structural element. Similarly, most of his poems are based on symbols such as the child and the king, large symbols which play little part in the details of their formal organization, but which merely give rise to meditations on innocence and true wealth or simple presentations of childhood experiences. In the course of a poem many lesser symbols may be introduced to illustrate the thought, and sometimes they are only convenient philosophical names for God, like "the Fountain" in *The Antici-pation*; at other times, however, the poet vitalizes them so that they excite the imagination as does the Spring, Stream, and Ocean symbolism in *Silence* (ll. 61–74). But his mind moves freely from one symbol to another, ignoring the subtle unifying force with which they could be invested, so that there are very few whole poems in which he uses a particular symbol throughout. Certainly, no poem by Traherne is sufficiently closely woven to afford the peculiar aesthetic pleasure of poems like Marvell's *On a Drop of Dew* which are miracles of symbolic design.

One reason for Traherne's failure to make each poem clearly an artistic unity is his refusal to accept severe restrictions. His mind reaches out further and further to embrace infinity, and he is happiest when working on a very large scale. Poems like *The Apprehension* and *Fullnesse* are comparatively meaningless in isolation, yet if one reads through all the thirty-seven poems from the Dobell Folio Manuscript in their original order, one cannot but be impressed by the continuity and logical arrange-ment of the thoughts in the total pattern; indeed, it has been suggested that these poems constitute a complete five-part meditation which fulfils all the major conditions of a Jesuit exercise.[41] Symbols and images, too, are often more significant in the structure of the series than in the structure of any one poem; for example, the water symbolism in *Silence* enriches the declaration in *The Estate* that

> as the spacious Main
> Doth all the Rivers, which it Drinks, return,
> Thy Love receivd doth make the Soul to burn,

which in turn enriches the meaning of the final stanza of *The Circulation*, where there is a similar use of water symbolism. Between Traherne and most other poets there is a difference like that between the novelist and the short story writer; he demands spaciousness and formal looseness and will not submit to strict economy and tight bonds.

At first sight the complex stanza forms which he often chooses, and no one of which he ever repeats in another poem, seem to contradict the statement that he refuses to accept severe restrictions. However, these forms generally do not appear to

---

41. J. M. Wallace, "Thomas Traherne and the Structure of Meditation", *English Literary History*, XXV (1958), 80.

act as restrictions to his thought or expression, both of which lack the concentration typical of metaphysical poetry. To him a stanza is not a limiting frame into which the thought is compressed, but merely a pleasant device to turn thought into verse, and the reader gains the impression of free-roaming religious reflections and aspirations flowing out easily and spontaneously into a chosen shape. This effect is obtained partly by his "inartistic" use of symbols, whereby his thought is liberated from sustained domination by any concrete symbol, and partly by the facility with which he multiplies enumerations or repeats ideas or catalogues virtually synonymous symbols:

> Ye hidden Nectars, which my GOD doth drink,
> Ye Heavenly Streams, ye Beams Divine,
> On which the Angels think,
> How Quick, how Strongly do ye shine![42]

"Quand la largeur du champ de conscience s'exagère, il est vain d'attendre que le poète resserre, condense, compose."[43]

It is partly Traherne's basic distrust of the seductive power and the possible obscurity of figurative language that makes him wary of tying his thought closely to a particular symbol to be used as an essential force in the shaping of a poem. Though his poetry is an intensely personal expression of individual passion, there is always a strongly didactic purpose behind the intimate revelations which he shares with his reader, a purpose which dictates the plainness of his language and the simplicity of his style. He is so determined that nothing shall come between himself and his reader that he is unhappy about using metaphor at all, while his occasional use of verbal paradox, as in the first line of *Eden* ("A learned and a Happy Ignorance"), is very unmetaphysical, for it expresses a pure wonder which suppresses perplexity. Too frequently he is not content to step aside and let symbols make their own impact. Sometimes they are introduced as comparisons after their meaning has already been stated, as in the lines

> God is Himself the Means,
> Wherby he doth exist:
> And as the Sun by Shining's clothd with Beams,

---

42. "Ye hidden Nectars", ll. 1–4.
43. Ellrodt, *op. cit.*, p. 389.

So from Himself to All His Glory Streams,
Who is a Sun, yet what Himself doth list.[44]

At other times the poet comments on or interprets their meaning after he has used them; at the end of *Bells* he feels compelled to emphasize thus the sufficiently obvious significance of the harmonious ringing of church bells:

We must unite
If we Delight
Would yield or feel, or any Excellence.

Traherne is easily carried away by his boundless energy and by his impetuous enthusiasm to proclaim that his reader, too, can share his ecstatic vision.

The beautiful but imperfect poem *Goodnesse*, the last in the Dobell Folio Manuscript, provides an interesting example of some of the literary strengths and weaknesses of Traherne's use of symbols. This poem depends on them for its impact far more than do most of his other poems and requires more careful reading, and in it he appears to make some attempt to realize the unifying power of symbols. One critic has even called *Goodnesse* a very obscure poem,[45] but it is not obscure to an imaginative reader who is familiar with traditional symbols and has become accustomed to Traherne's symbolic vision as expressed in the previous poems from the same manuscript.

Goodnesse opens with an abrupt statement of the chief idea, "The Bliss of other Men is my Delight", which is then expanded and illustrated by a reference to Ocean and water-drop symbolism.[46] However, Traherne evidently feels that this illustration is of itself inadequate, because he offers two more in the second stanza, both based on light symbolism, in which it is impossible to separate the literal from the symbolic. The mystic gives the impression that he is contemplating first a vineyard and then the starry heavens, meditating on the beauty which, he thinks, they both reflect from the sun, and on the miracle of his personal possession of them all; nevertheless, the poem's opening line and the statement in line 5 that "The Face of GOD is Goodness unto all" point to a much deeper interpretation. God is the

---

44. *The Anticipation*, ll. 50–54.
45. Jean-Jacques Denonain, *Thèmes et Formes de la Poésie "Métaphysique": Etude d'un aspect de la Littérature Anglaise au Dix-Septième Siècle* (Paris, 1956), p. 267.
46. Lines 7–12 are discussed previously (see pp. 53–54).

"Light", the "Beams", the "Greater Beauty", or the "Sun", and each person is a vine in the Lord's vineyard or a star in His heavens reflecting the divine glory and multiplying Traherne's spiritual inheritance.

The apt symbolism of stanzas 1 and 2, with its cosmic sweep embracing sea, earth, and sky, is satisfying to the reader; but characteristically Traherne is not satisfied that his symbols speak forcefully enough, and besides, it gives him deep pleasure to let his thoughts wander freely along familiar tracks. In stanzas 3 and 4 he therefore makes explicit what is already implicit, appropriately placing the greatest emphasis on the vital connection between bliss and goodness, and expressing in exclamations his wonder and delight. Nevertheless, these stanzas have loose symbolic links with the others, for the words "reign" and "Sovereign" evoke the image of God calling thousands to His throne and the implication behind the verb "crown", while the statement that "His Burning Lov the Bliss of all doth prove" is a subtle glance back to the sun symbolism of stanza 2 and a preparation for its recapitulation.

A poet more concerned with purely artistic values would probably have placed the rich imagery of stanzas 5 and 6 directly after stanza 2 without intervening explanations. In the first half of stanza 5 there is again a perfect fusion of the literal and the symbolic as seen on earth and in sky, and the thoughts of the previous stanzas are developed more fully. The Sun's maturing heat causes the responsive "Bleeding Vines" to bring forth fruit to be food and drink for Traherne's soul in a holy communion with the Divine One and all His images who, like stars, are constant assurances of His immediate presence.[47] The second half of the stanza is on a more purely symbolic level. Heaven is pictured as the home of perfected human beings, who there are "better Vines" in the Lord's vineyard or "Lillies", white flowers of light, in His garden.[48] By the warmth and favour of the Sun they produce for Traherne's enjoyment, even in his earthly state, "Far Better Wines" than those produced on earth, and yield the "pleasant Odors" of their services to his soul.[49]

The final stanza is an exalted vision of "The Highest Joys

---

47. See the section on spiritual touch, pp. 13–14, this volume.

48. Cf. Vaughan, "Though with no Lilie, stay with me!" (*Cock-crowing*, l. 48), and Cowley, "The Virgin Lillies in their White, / Are clad but with the Lawn of almost Naked Light" (*Hymn to Light*, ll. 75–76).

49. See l. 23, and the section on spiritual odour, pp. 14-18 of this book.

[God's] Goodness did prepare"—all those in whom, as in Traherne, lives the image of His goodness,[50] no matter whether on earth or in Heaven. The simile comparing their united love with the vastness and sweetness of "Seas / Of Nectar and Ambrosia" recalls the ocean symbolism of stanza 1 and the "Drink", "Meat", and "pleasant Odors" of stanza 5, while the metaphors identifying eyes with stars and lips with grapes afford imagistic links with stanzas 2 and 5. These metaphors are not mere fanciful repetition, however, for they add greater depth to the whole poem. Since in many previous poems Traherne uses the eye as a symbol for man's soul,[51] and since "soft and Swelling Grapes" is for him an unusually sensuous image, it seems probable that in stanza 2 and in the first half of stanza 5, where the literal and the symbolic are fused, he expresses his spiritual joy in material things, especially the human body, by his imagery of the vineyard, and his joy in spiritual things, especially the human soul, by his imagery of the starry heavens. Traherne's special gift of illuminating the spiritual by the sensuous and at the same time spiritualizing the sensuous is finely illustrated in *Goodnesse*. The image of the "soft and Swelling Grapes" is followed immediately by a metaphor identifying human tongues with "A Quire of Blessed and Harmonious Songs" and thus evoking the idea of an angelic chorus. This is the first time a musical image is introduced, but it is particularly appropriate that a poem whose principal underlying theme is the spiritual marriage between God and His Church should end with such great emphasis on joyful harmony.

Readers critical of Traherne's artistic imperfections could wish that his symbolic vision of the perfect harmony of all things had been put into practice in the creation of his poems, which are always marred by faulty structure or clumsy expression. *Goodnesse* is constructed far more neatly than most of his poems, and is a fairly adequate expression of his experience of God's immanence; yet stanzas 3 and 4 are largely unnecessary repetition, and a better poet would have been able to intensify the immediate impact of the symbols in the other stanzas, perhaps by presenting them more dramatically instead of relying on reflective statement. Generally speaking, Traherne's verse can be called "poetry" mainly because of the beauty of its thoughts, and it is probably

---

50. See ll. 29–30, 69.
51. See previously, pp. 23–28.

true that "if we are not already in some respect sympathetic to his vision on other grounds, the poetry will not make us intimately share in it".[52] However, his poems are not devoid of beauty of expression, and this chapter has shown that many of his artistic faults are virtues when they are judged from a wider point of view than the solely aesthetic. No other style could give such a clear reflection of his fascinating personality as does the rhapsodic spontaneity of his verse, for the reader feels that he is watching poetry-in-the-making unfolding before him and thoughts freely expanding to embrace infinity.

---

52. K. W. Salter, *Thomas Traherne: Mystic and Poet* (London, 1964), p. 119.

CONCLUSION

"MY SPIRIT"

... THE MOST GLORIOUS POETRY THAT HAS EVER BEEN COMMUNICATED
TO THE WORLD IS PROBABLY A FEEBLE SHADOW OF THE ORIGINAL
CONCEPTIONS OF THE POET.

(SHELLEY: *A Defence of Poetry*)

"As HERBERT EMBODIED ALL THE THEMES OF THE POETS OF content, Traherne was the seventeenth-century climax of the poets of aspiration."[1] In his introductory poem, *The Author to the Critical Peruser*, he makes it clear that what he aspires to, for himself and all mankind, is the felicity of spiritual kingship, which he is sure can be found only by seeing and enjoying the Divine as revealed in all God's works, and especially in the beauty and usefulness of one's body and the infinite capacities of one's soul, God's image. In other poems, Traherne further develops this theory. According to him, man's insatiableness is the proof of his potential royalty, and instead of being checked or curbed it must be transferred to the spiritual realm and allowed freedom to pursue the promptings of nature until it becomes a passion for the infinite that finds its fulfilment in the spiritual possession of God and all things at once within the soul of man. When he is in this exalted state man is closest to the Infinite One, because most like Him, and he is most pleasing to Him, because only thus can man fully play his part in the great circulation of all things from God to him, and back to God through his appreciation, thanksgiving, and love. However, in order to fulfil his passion for the infinite, man must exercise his spiritual senses, particularly his sight, which at its highest level of operation includes within itself all the other senses. Such is the aspiring vision that gives life to Traherne's poems and dictates his use of symbols.

---

1. Marjorie Hope Nicolson, *The Breaking of the Circle: Studies in the Effect of the "New Science" upon Seventeenth-Century Poetry* (rev. ed.; New York, 1960), p. 196.

Such a firm conviction of the exalted position to which man can and should attain tends to make Traherne's mysticism curiously homocentric or even egocentric, and his most comprehensive poem, *My Spirit*, is an attempt to describe a mystical experience in which his primary concern is not with God but with his own soul when it is most like God. The position of *My Spirit* after *Silence* in the Dobell Folio Manuscript indicates that, characteristically, he attributes this experience to himself as an infant; and if it were not for the discovery in 1964 of *Select Meditations*, in which it is described as a personal experience of his adulthood,[2] the sceptical reader might have claimed that Traherne manufactured it from his imaginative philosophy of the ideal state of childhood. However, the reader who is sympathetic to his vision needs no proof of the direct authenticity of the thoughts and feelings expressed in this remarkable poem which, standing at the very heart of Traherne's mysticism, provides an excellent illustration of the most important points concerning the special way in which he uses conventional mystical symbolism.

My Spirit opens with a brief, arresting statement, "My Naked Simple Life was I", which plunges the reader directly into the midst of an experience in which the very essence of the human soul is revealed in all its glorious "simplicity", or indivisibility, as pure "Act". Traherne dares to assert that on earth it is possible to reach that state of absolute perfection in which all the potentialities of the soul are actualized so that its sight, indistinguishable from itself, is powerful and limitless like the sun's beams shining "Upon the Earth, the Sea, the Skie"—a typical list of vast objects.[3] The purity of his soul is its boundlessness, its ability to feel and hold "all Things" "as in a Bowl": "My Essence was Capacitie." The "Bowl" simile and the word "Capacitie" remind the reader of his statements in the previous poem, *Silence*: "My Bosom was an Ocean", and

A vast and Infinit Capacitie,
Did make my Bosom like the Deitie.

This "Capacitie" results from a total unification of his whole

2. See p. vi, this volume, for quotation.
3. Cf. Traherne's assertions in *The Preparative* that his soul was

A vital Sun that round about did *ray*
All Life and Sence,
A Naked Simple Pure *Intelligence.*

being on a spiritual level; he is not aware of the separate activity of his physical or spiritual senses, for they are part of the spiritual "Thought" that is his soul. The boldest lines in this stanza are the final three, in which, while referring to his own soul, Traherne explicitly uses that particular kind of space symbolism traditionally reserved strictly for God alone—the Sphere Whose centre is everywhere and Whose circumference is nowhere. However, this virtual identification with God of his soul during the mystical experience has already been implied by the hint that his soul is the Sun and the Ocean because it is all "Act", as God is.[4]

All the main ideas have now been introduced, but they need further clarification; and so determined is Traherne to make his reader see his meaning that stanza 2 is extraordinarily unpoetic in the plainness of its expression. His difficulty in maintaining his complicated stanza pattern is only too obvious, but the thoughts which he turns into verse are very poetic. They relate the sphere symbol to the unified soul's omnipresence by means of spiritual sight, which actualizes all the soul's potentialities so that it becomes "all Ey, all Act, all Sight" possessing the Protean quality of light and thus able to identify itself with any object it sees. Here again the poet uses for his own soul symbols which he elsewhere uses for God; in *Felicity* it is God Who is described as a "Sphere of Lov" Which is

> all full of Sight,
> All Soul and Life, an Ey most bright,
> All Light and Lov.

It would be impossible to emphasize God's immanence in man more strongly; hence it is natural that Traherne should so apprehend His immanence in the material world that in his nature imagery in particular there is often a fusion of sense and spirit, of the literal and the symbolic.[5] His poetry is essentially a poetry of immanence.

Stanzas 3 and 4 deal with further aspects of his soul's mysterious omnipresence. It operates in a realm outside time, in a kind of illuminated eternal present in which the outer and inner worlds become one. This eternal present is infinitely extended, allowing him to satisfy his desire for infinite spiritual

---

4. Cf. "[God's] Essence is all Act" (*The Anticipation*, l. 91).
5. See pp. 107–10, 118–19, 124–25, 125, 126.

possession of all the objects of the material world; moreover, so vivid are the images within his spirit that they seem to be the outer objects themselves, yet at the same time inseparably united with himself. Spirit, mind, and sense are so fused that there is no definite distinction between the spiritual, the intellectual, and the material; Traherne's spiritual world tends to be a Platonic ideal copy of the material world, whose inner presence is more real to him than its physical presence.[6] Furthermore, distance is totally abolished in his inner world where even the most remote objects, like the sun or the "utmost Star", are present in the very centre of his indivisible being, "the Apple of [his] Eye". He feels himself truly to be a sphere whose centre is everywhere and whose circumference is nowhere.

There is never any arrogance, however, in the mystic's bold assertions of the exaltation of man, but rather a reverential wonder that God has deigned thus to exalt His creature. Traherne makes very daring claims because his confidence is based on deep personal experience, and in the first half of stanza 5 he expresses his delighted wonder characteristically by a series of exclamations in which the light and sphere symbols are again applied to his own spirit, "An Image of the Deitie". Cautious as usual, Philip Traherne altered the exclamation "My Soul a Spirit infinit!" to the considerably tamer line, "My Soul a Spirit wide and bright!"—thus destroying its significance and revealing a refusal to face the fact that the theme of *My Spirit* and of most of Thomas's other poems is the infinity of the soul's essence which makes it a "Bower of Bliss". In the second half of this stanza the poet implies the connection between infinity and love. It is a love for God's creatures similar to His own love for them that makes it possible for the soul to actualize its infinite potentialities by reaching out to embrace all things simultaneously, as God does; and it is primarily the soul's close similarity to its Creator that ties the bond of loving communion between the human and the Divine. Significantly, Traherne even here prefers to describe himself as the "Son and friend of God" rather than as the bride of God, for his mysticism, though passionate, is more intellectual and less personal than that of most other Christian mystics. In his poetry there is a consistent tendency to elevate man towards the position of God the Father, and the created world towards the

---

6. Thus at times he seems to be a little more concrete than usual when he is writing of mental images, e.g., in *Thoughts* III, ll. 37–44.

position of God the Son;[7] thus the experience on which *My Spirit* is based is not mystical union with Christ, but mystical union with the world, which seems to take His place as the Mediator between God and man.

Stanza 6 provides the clearest evidence of the difficulty of trying to express the inexpressible.[8] If the soul is infinite and eternal, how can it be a sphere, or any other shape? Hence the paradox of an "Orb of Joy" which yet was "not a Sphere". The mystic's experience beyond the realm of logic forces him to conclude that his soul is like a circle of perfection, but that it is a circle extended everywhere instantaneously, yet at the same time wholly concentrated or centred in every point. Its powers are limitless.

This deep contemplation of the mysterious nature of the spirit again moves Traherne to exclamatory utterance, and since he now reaches the highest point of ecstatic exhilaration, nearly half of the final stanza consists of a list of vocatives addressing his soul by titles which in view of the previous stanzas are seen to be virtually synonymous and which combine the light and eye symbols with the space symbolism of sphere, air, and world. Such exclamatory repetition of exalted ideas and of the large, general symbols associated with them is typical of this mystic, whose enthusiastic and aspiring spirit can be content with nothing short of the infinity of space, time, number, and variety as expressed by God in the creation of the universe and by man in his mental recreation of it. The concrete and the particular are foreign to his expansive soul which he feels is a "Power infinit", in its highest moments able to become an infinite "Act" with a kingly possession of all things by means of a spiritual marriage with them. His passion for the Infinite One is indistinguishable from his passion for the unbounded in everything and his emotive need to elevate everything to the infinite; thus in his poems both God and man are referred to as Eye, Sun, Ocean, Space, and King, while the material creation is spiritualized by an illuminated vision. Occasionally, as at the end of *My Spirit*, there is a brief reminder of the obscuring veil of sin which eclipses that great sun, the human soul, and all its inner objects; but nearly all of the poetry of Thomas Traherne has the freshness and joyousness of one who sees Felicity with the eyes of a child.

---

7. See pp. 52–58, 98, 99–100, 104–6.
8. Lines 86–96 are discussed on pp. 67–68 of this volume.

BIBLIOGRAPHY

This is not a complete Traherne bibliography. The section entitled *Writings by Traherne* lists all consulted editions of his works. The section entitled *Writings About Traherne* lists all those consulted writings which contain more than mere references to Traherne, and thus includes many writings which do not deal exclusively with him. The section entitled *General Reference Material* lists only material which was of considerable assistance to the author.

Writings by Traherne

BELL, H. I. (ed.). *Traherne's Poems of Felicity.* Oxford, 1910.

MARGOLIOUTH, H. M. (ed.). *Thomas Traherne: Centuries, Poems, and Thanksgivings.* 2 vols. Oxford, 1958.

RIDLER, ANNE (ed.). *Thomas Traherne: Poems, Centuries and Three Thanksgivings.* Oxford Standard Authors. London, 1966.

TRAHERNE, THOMAS. *Centuries of Meditations,* ed. Bertram Dobell. Reprint with introduction by John Hayward. London, 1950.

——. *A Serious and Pathetical Contemplation of the Mercies of God, in several most Devout and Sublime Thanksgivings for the Same,* ed. R. Daniells. (University of Toronto Studies, "Philology and Literature Series", No. 12.) Toronto, 1941.

WADE, GLADYS I. (ed.). *The Poetical Works of Thomas Traherne.* London, 1932.

Writings About Traherne

BEACHCROFT, T. O. "Traherne and the Cambridge Platonists", *Dublin Review,* CLXXXVI (1930), 278–90.

——. "Traherne, and the Doctrine of Felicity", *Criterion,* IX (1930), 291–307.

BOTTRALL, M. "Traherne's Praise of the Creation", *Critical Quarterly,* I (1959), 126–33.

BULLETT, GERALD. *The English Mystics.* London, 1950.

BUSH, DOUGLAS. *English Literature in the Earlier Seventeenth Century 1600–1660.* Oxford, 1945.

CLEMENTS, A. L. "On the Mode and Meaning of Traherne's Mystical Poetry: 'The Preparative' ", *Studies in Philology*, LXI (1964), 500–21.

COLBY, F. L. "Thomas Traherne and Henry More", *Modern Language Notes*, LXII (1947), 490–92.

COLIE, R. L. "Thomas Traherne and the Infinite: The Ethical Compromise", *Huntington Library Quarterly*, XXI (1957), 69–82.

DENONAIN, JEAN-JACQUES. *Thèmes et Formes de la Poésie "Métaphysique"*: *Etude d'un aspect de la Littérature Anglaise au Dix-Septième Siècle*. Paris, 1956.

ELIOT, T. S. "Mystic and Politician as Poet: Vaughan, Traherne, Marvell, Milton", *Listener*, III (1930), 590–91.

ELLRODT, ROBERT. *L'inspiration personnelle et l'esprit du temps chez les poètes métaphysiques anglais*, première partie, tome II. Paris, 1960.

———. "Le Message de Thomas Traherne, Apôtre de la Félicité", *Cahiers du Sud*, XXXI (1950), 434–56.

FLEMING, W. K. *Mysticism in Christianity*. London, 1913.

GILBERT, A. H. "Thomas Traherne as Artist", *Modern Language Quarterly*, VIII (1947), 319–41, 435–47.

GRANDVOINET, R. "Thomas Traherne and the Doctrine of Felicity", *Etudes de Lettres*, XIII (1939), 164–78.

GRIERSON, HERBERT J. C. *The First Half of the Seventeenth Century*. Edinburgh and London, 1906.

GRIGSON, G. "The Transports of Thomas Traherne", *Bookman*, LXXXII (1932), 250.

HALL, W. C. "Poetical Works of Thomas Traherne", *Manchester Quarterly*, October 1904, pp. 376–82.

HEPBURN, R. W. "Thomas Traherne: The Nature and Dignity of Imagination", *Cambridge Journal*, VI (1953), 725–34.

HERMAN, E. *The Meaning and Value of Mysticism*. 3rd ed. London, 1922.

HOBHOUSE, S. "A Poet's Resurrection", *Spectator*, DCLIV (1936), 804.

HODGSON, GERALDINE E. *English Mystics*. London and Oxford, 1922.

HOLMES, ELIZABETH. *Henry Vaughan and the Hermetic Philosophy*. Oxford, 1932.

HOWARTH, R. G. " 'Felicity' in Traherne", *Notes and Queries*, CXCIII (1948), 249–50.

IREDALE, Q. *Thomas Traherne*. Oxford, 1935.

ITRAT-HUSAIN. *The Mystical Element in the Metaphysical Poets of the Seventeenth Century*. Edinburgh and London, 1948.

JONES, RUFUS M. *Spiritual Reformers in the 16th and 17th Centuries*. London, 1914.

JONES, W. L. "Thomas Traherne and the Religious Poetry of the Seventeenth Century", *Quarterly Review*, CC (1904), 437–64.

LEISHMAN, J. B. *The Metaphysical Poets: Donne, Herbert, Vaughan, Traherne*. New York, 1963.

LOCK, W. "An English Mystic", *Constructive Quarterly*, I (1913), 826–36.

MAHOOD, M. M. *Poetry and Humanism*. London, 1950.

MARKS, C. L. "Thomas Traherne and Cambridge Platonism", *PMLA*, LXXXI (1966), 521–34.

MARSHALL, W. H. "Thomas Traherne and The Doctrine of Original Sin", *Modern Language Notes*, LXXIII (1958), 161–65.

MARTZ, LOUIS L. *The Paradise Within: Studies in Vaughan, Traherne, and Milton*. New Haven and London, 1964.

MASSINGHAM, H. "A Note on Thomas Traherne", *New Statesman*, IV (1914), 271–72.

MORE, P. E. "Thomas Traherne", *Nation*, LXXXVIII (1909), 160–62.

NAYLOR, E. W. "Three Seventeenth Century Poet-Parsons and Music", *Proceedings of the Musical Association*, LIV (1928), 93–113.

NICOLSON, MARJORIE HOPE. *The Breaking of the Circle: Studies in the Effect of the "New Science" upon Seventeenth-Century Poetry*. Rev. ed. New York, 1960.

———. *Mountain Gloom and Mountain Glory: The Development of the Aesthetics of the Infinite*. New York, 1959.

OSBORN, J. M. "A New Traherne Manuscript", *London Times Literary Supplement*, 8 October 1964, p. 928.

OSMOND, PERCY H. *The Mystical Poets of the English Church*. London and New York, 1919.

PARKES, S. T. H. "A Devout Hedonist: The Riches of Thomas Traherne", *To-day*, IX (1922), 59–62.

RIDLON, H. G. "The Function of the 'Infant-Ey' in Traherne's Poetry", *Studies in Philology*, LXI (1964), 627–39.

SALTER, K. W. *Thomas Traherne: Mystic and Poet*. London, 1964.

SHERER, G. R. "More and Traherne", *Modern Language Notes*, XXXIV (1919), 49–50.

SPURGEON, CAROLINE F. E. *Mysticism in English Literature*. Cambridge Manuals of Science and Literature. Cambridge, 1913.

STRANKS, C. J. *Anglican Devotion: Studies in the Spiritual Life of the Church of England between the Reformation and the Oxford Movement*. London, 1961.

"Thomas Traherne", *Spectator*, CXXIV (1920), 84–85.

THOMPSON, E. N. S. "Mysticism in Seventeenth-Century English Literature", *Studies in Philology*, XVIII (1921), 170–231.

———. "The Philosophy of Thomas Traherne", *Philological Quarterly*, VIII (1929), 97–112.

TOWERS, F. "Thomas Traherne: His Outlook on Life", *Nineteenth Century*, LXXXVII (1920), 1024–30.

WADE, GLADYS I. "St. Thomas Aquinas and Thomas Traherne", *Blackfriars*, XII (1931), 666–73.

———. *Thomas Traherne: A Critical Biography*. Princeton, 1944.

———. "Thomas Traherne as 'Divine Philosopher' ", *Hibbert Journal,* XXXII (1934), 400–408.

———. "Traherne and the Spiritual Value of Nature Study", *London Quarterly and Holborn Review,* CLIX (1934), 243–45.

WAHL, J. "Poèmes de Thomas Traherne", *Mesures,* 15 April 1936, pp. 59–89.

WALLACE, J. M. "Thomas Traherne and the Structure of Meditation", *English Literary History,* XXV (1958), 79–89.

WHITE, HELEN C. *The Metaphysical Poets: A Study in Religious Experience.* New York, 1936.

WILLCOX, L. C. "A Joyous Mystic", *North American Review,* CXCIII (1911), 893–904.

WILLETT, GLADYS E. *Traherne (An Essay).* Cambridge, 1919.

WILLSON, C. H. S. "Traherne and Wordsworth", *London Quarterly and Holborn Review,* CLXIV (1939), 355–58.

WILLY, MARGARET. *Life Was Their Cry.* London, 1950.

———. "Thomas Traherne: 'Felicity's Perfect Lover' ", *English,* XII (1959), 210–15.

———. *Three Metaphysical Poets.* Supplement to *British Book News,* No. 134 on Writers and Their Work. London, 1961.

WILSON, A. D. L. "A Neglected Mystic: Thomas Traherne", *Poetry Review,* XVI (1925), 11–12, 97–104, 178–82.

WRIGHT, JUDITH. "Reading Thomas Traherne", in *Five Senses: Selected Poems by Judith Wright.* Sydney, 1963.

General Reference Material

EWER, MARY ANITA. *A Survey of Mystical Symbolism.* London, 1933.

UNDERHILL, EVELYN. *Mysticism: A Study in the Nature and Development of Man's Spiritual Consciousness.* 12th ed. rev. London, 1930.